*Struggle with God
and Overcome*

Struggle with God and Overcome

William Lam

Foreword by David Ling

WIPF & STOCK • Eugene, Oregon

STRUGGLE WITH GOD AND OVERCOME

Copyright © 2022 William Lam. All rights reserved. Except for brief quotations in critical publications or reviews, no part of this book may be reproduced in any manner without prior written permission from the publisher. Write: Permissions, Wipf and Stock Publishers, 199 W. 8th Ave., Suite 3, Eugene, OR 97401.

Wipf & Stock
An Imprint of Wipf and Stock Publishers
199 W. 8th Ave., Suite 3
Eugene, OR 97401

www.wipfandstock.com

PAPERBACK ISBN: 978-1-6667-4298-5
HARDCOVER ISBN: 978-1-6667-4299-2
EBOOK ISBN: 978-1-6667-4300-5

08/08/22

All Scripture quotations, unless otherwise indicated, are taken from the Holy Bible, New International Version®, NIV®. Copyright ©1973, 1978, 1984, 2011 by Biblica, Inc.™ Used by permission of Zondervan. All rights reserved worldwide. www.zondervan.com The "NIV" and "New International Version" are trademarks registered in the United States Patent and Trademark Office by Biblica, Inc.™

To my parents, Grace and James Lam

Contents

List of Tables | ix
List of Figures | xi
Foreword | xiii
Preface | xv

The Reasons Behind | 1
Mysteries and Adventure | 3
Tenacious Challenger | 6
Dubious Resort | 9
Blessings Misplaced | 11
Isaac's Patriarchal Benediction | 14
Gorge of Jabbok | 16
Watershed Moment | 20
Life Stages | 23
Turn of Events | 27
Methodology | 30
Shechem | 32
Rachel and Reuben | 36
Leaving the Brothers | 38
Judah and Tamar | 40
Two Clans | 43
The Kingdoms | 46

Old and New Testament Parallels | 49
Sheaves and Stars | 51
At Potiphar's House | 54
Cupbearer and Baker | 57
Abandoned | 61
Pharaoh's Dreams | 64
Joseph and Jesus | 69
Staging | 77
Famine | 80
First Reunion | 81
First Coming | 85
Second Reunion | 90
Benjamin | 96
Second Coming | 98
Motif and Auspice | 102
The Wrestled Blessing | 105
Patriarchal Narratives | 111
Tribal Blessings | 113
Struggle with God and Overcome | 118
Blessedness versus Happiness | 120

Bibliography | 123

List of Tables

Table 1. Traits from sheaves and stars | 53

Table 2. Traits from Potiphar's house | 56

Table 3. Traits from the cupbearer and baker | 59

Table 4. Traits from abandoned | 62

Table 5. Traits from Pharaoh's dreams | 67

Table 6. Summary of Joseph's signature traits arranged in NT order | 69

Table 7. Summary of Joseph and Jesus signature traits comparison | 75

Table 8. Characteristics of the first reunion | 84

Table 9. Comparison of Joseph's first reunion and Jesus' first coming | 88

Table 10. Characteristics of the second reunion | 95

Table 11. Comparison of the second reunion and Jesus' second coming | 100

List of Figures

Figure 1. Jacob's exile | 24

Figure 2. Jacob's life timeline | 26

Figure 3. Test of the elected | 35

Figure 4. Forming of the tribes | 37

Figure 5. Jacob's life second stage | 39

Figure 6. Bifurcation of family clans | 42

Figure 7. Jacob's family tree | 43

Figure 8. Two clans and signature messages | 78

Figure 9. Comparing Joseph's first reunion with Jesus' first coming | 89

Figure 10. Comparing Joseph's second reunion with Jesus' second coming | 101

Figure 11. Spiritual implications of Joseph's and Judah's clan | 104

Figure 12. Jacob's life summary | 107

Figure 13. Major events in Jacob's mission years | 108

Figure 14. Significance of Jacob's mission years | 109

Foreword

EVERY CHRISTIAN WHO IS serious about the faith must have experienced fierce battles with God, especially when facing difficult and bewildering circumstances. It is commonly believed that faith in God brings blessings such as happiness and peace. In this book, the author offers a different perspective on blessing that transcends the conventional interpretation.

In the first half of his life as an opportunist, Jacob hunted for blessings at every possible opportunity, even in dire circumstances. At the night in the ford of Jabbok, facing the possibility of losing all his hard-earned fortune and even his life, Jacob grappled with a stranger. Unfazed by the hip injury from the wrestling match, Jacob persisted till daybreak and insisted on a blessing before letting the man go. The Bible is reticent about the contents of the blessing that called for a change of Jacob's name to Israel, an unusual move for a life-changing blessing when every other blessing on Jacob was spelled out clearly. The author attempts to explore the contents and meanings of this wrestled blessing from passages in the Bible.

The wrestling match has changed Jacob's life physically and spiritually. Physically, Jacob has become crippled for the rest of his life. Spiritually, Jacob has now changed from grappling with man, as the name Jacob suggests, to wrestling with God, as the name Israel indicates. Jacob's life afterward testifies to this watershed moment.

Many events, almost all of which are tragic, followed the wrestling match. To make sense of these tragic events following the preceding blessing, the author first captures the essential messages, called signature traits, of these events and then forms a framework by interconnecting these signature traits. To interpret the meanings of the framework, the author associates the people, actions, and incidents with the corresponding ones in the New Testament by examining similar signature traits between those in the stories and the New Testament. The association with the events in the New Testament functions to demonstrate that the thirty-three years of Jacob's life after the wrestled blessing foreshadow what eventually happened in the New Testament, shedding light on God's salvation plan for humanity. Furthermore, illumination from the biblical account of Jacob's life reveals the superiority of God's blessings over people's expectation of blessings. Genuine blessedness is not limited to materialistic abundance but goes beyond and achieves renewal of life. This divine notion of blessedness has been in God's salvation plan for all since the fall of Adam.

The renewal of life is a lifelong process, which necessarily progresses from the stumbling of infancy, the setback of adolescence, to the struggle and distress of adulthood, thereby we learn, overcome, and eventually achieve victory—the whole measure of the fullness of Christ. This is the key message the author wishes to convey.

Through the book's investigative study, I appreciate the author's in-depth understanding and refreshing interpretations of the events in the Bible, which lead to many spiritual insights. Because the Bible is God-breathed, our continuing search and meditation will undoubtedly lead to more discoveries of God's rich and profound wisdom and plan.

Rev. David Ling
Senior Pastor Emeritus, serving forty-plus years
in the San Francisco Bay Area and Hong Kong

Preface

ALTHOUGH THOUSANDS OF YEARS old, the life stories of Jacob are still applicable in modern days. People come to God for blessings and expect blessings to manifest in prosperity, fame, health, and peace. Jacob, a perennial blessing chaser, was the trailblazer on this path, fighting for his birthright while still in the womb. God had been with Jacob, promising him blessings and protecting him from harm. Then all of a sudden, calamities fell upon him after he wrestled a blessing at the ford of Jabbok. What happened? Did not God bless Jacob? This mystery should not be overlooked because Jacob was a patriarch of the nation of Israel and God was directly involved. Furthermore, the message behind the mystery should be spiritually significant.

This book came as a result of my sermon preparations on some of the Old Testament stories. It started out as a lingering question that has since led to more questions and a tantalizing suspicion that these questions were all hooked to a large piece of mystery. After about a year of study, research, and meditation, I summarize my findings in this book, which gives a glimpse of the mystery. I hope this book opens the door to a better understanding of what blessedness is.

A picture is worth a thousand words. I believe tables and diagrams oftentimes elucidate better than words, where, in a diagram, the positioning, grouping, and connecting by arrows of words and objects depict a mental picture amicable for

Preface

recollection. Thus, this book has an uncharacteristically higher density of diagrams and tables than most books of a similar genre. In the end, I hope the diagrams help the reader visualize and absorb the intricate interplays and comparisons between the various events and protagonists.

My initial interest and subsequent pursuit of the subject during today's unprecedentedly tumultuous time would not be possible without the providence of God, who granted me insights, confidence, and persistence to complete the book. Further, I thank my wife, Serene, and daughters, Rachel and Priscilla, for maintaining a loving home that refreshes the sagging spirit and replenishes the empty stomach. I appreciate my illustration artist in residence, Priscilla Lam, who in her innate talent made the diagrams pleasing to the eyes and clear to the mind. I would like to acknowledge the reviewers who amid their busy schedules tackled the rough draft and offered valuable encouragement and critiques that have shaped and refined the manuscript. Fuller Theological Seminary provided me with access to its online library, which proves to be the singularly most valuable vehicle in my research, for which I am indebted. I acknowledge iBible Maps (https://ibiblemaps.com/) for its extensive and lucid resources, which prove to be valuable in my study and research. Further, I appreciate Paul Fogg of iBible Maps for his generosity in giving permission for the use of foundational geographical materials in my book. Finally, I would like to thank Wipf and Stock Publishers for taking on the project, Matt Wimer, George Callihan, and the staff for their professionalism in making the publishing process smooth.

May 2022
Pleasanton, California

The Reasons Behind

SUFFERING IS INEVITABLY A part of life, and another part of life is eager to seek out the reasons behind suffering. Many causes exist to inflict suffering. Despite centuries of effort from the brilliant minds of philosophers and theologians, no satisfying answers have been found. The pain from suffering can be beyond words, however cogent and soothing. The perfect answer lies in God. Only God can supernaturally heal the wound and comfort the soul. In the book of Job, Job's friends attempted to rescue him from the pain through words and reasoning but succeeded only in rubbing salt into the wound. However, when God answered Job with more unanswerable questions, Job's spirit was awakened and healed. God's presence, even surrounded by impossible questions, is the perfect answer to suffering.

Nevertheless, answers to some sufferings are understandable and discoverable. The cause for Job's calamities is understandable: it is the work of Satan, whom God allowed to test Job. That the cause of Job's suffering is made known to all readers of the Bible but Job himself is a profound divine principle for all to ponder. Another principle about suffering is hidden in the life of Jacob. Jacob chased after blessings ever since he was in the womb, and God blessed him wherever he went. He prospered like Isaac and Abraham. However, unlike Job's experience, when Jacob encountered God in the wrestling match, his fortune seemed to take an adverse turn. His daughter was raped, two of his sons murdered innocent villagers, his favorite son disappeared, God slew two of his grandchildren, and famine threatened to wipe out his family. What is the cause of these troubles? Although the Bible does not explicitly state it, it is discoverable from detailed and rigorous analyses of the events under the spotlight of the New Testament.

It is mind-boggling to discover that the miserable thirty-three years in Jacob's life turned out to be an ultimate blessing from God. God bestowed Jacob the gift of living out the microcosm of God's plan of salvation for humanity spanning thousands of years—"Who can fathom the mind of the Lord?" (Isa 40:13).

Mysteries and Adventure

JACOB WAS BORN COMPETITIVE, always striving for the gold of blessings, winning matches against twin brother, Esau, uncle Laban, and even God. However, Jacob's fortune seemed to take a nosedive after he won the wrestling match with God at the gorge of Jabbok, where he insisted on getting a blessing. Before the wrestling match, Jacob got whatever he wanted, taking the birthright and patriarchal blessings from Esau and a massive amount of property from Laban. However, after the wrestling match, everything seemed to go against him. His only daughter, Dinah, was raped. Two of his sons, Simeon and Levi, schemed to kill and plunder a village in the name of circumcision. His beloved wife, Rachel, died while giving birth. His eldest son, Reuben, slept with his concubine. God struck down his two grandsons. He lost his favorite son, Joseph. And a famine threatened his family. God had anticipated Jacob's change in fortune—for better, not worse!—that God asked him to change his name to Israel.

Jacob's story is relevant in modern days: who doesn't want blessings from God? Reflecting on daily life, people frequently see more blights than blessings. Even when living is good and comfortable, people want more, so much as to wrestle blessings from God. The life story of Jacob, who devoted his entire life to seeking blessings, by whatever means it might take, is, therefore, a valuable lesson for all.

Didn't Jacob ask for a blessing at the end of the wrestling match? So, what happened? Although the Bible does not reveal the contents of that blessing, Jacob's life stories afterward are there for all to contemplate its meanings. Three cores of questions are in order. First, are these tragic stories all tied to the wrestled blessing? If so, do they relate to each other under a common theme? What is the wrestled blessing all about? Second, do blessings come to satisfy only the materialist needs, or do they carry spiritual messages? Finally, could a blessing necessarily bring the commonly acknowledged benefits, such as health, wealth, wisdom, and ultimately happiness? In other words, can a blessed person's life be full of disappointment, frustrations, and grief? Then, what is a blessing?

Before seeking answers to the above mysteries, textual meanings of cornerstone events in Jacob's biography need to be resolved, the nexus among them understood. The cornerstone events are the Shechem incident, Rachel's death, Reuben's indiscretion, the story of Judah and Tamar, and the selling of Joseph and his reunions with the family in Egypt.

It is a challenging task. First, the meanings and connections among some cornerstone stories are blurry. Scholars have long questioned the relevancy of the tale of Judah and Tamar, which is inserted in the middle of Joseph's story. Aside from a historical account, the massacre at Shechem can have many different and ambiguous interpretations, such as the nonchalance of Jacob's attitude toward Dinah's rape expressed as his hatred toward Leah, or violence, deception, and usury of sacred ceremony by the two sons, or even the unfairness of God. A fundamental question is: Is there necessarily a central theme among the cornerstone events in Jacob's life?

Second, there are many seemingly random snippets interspersed around the cornerstone events, which, aside from historical notes, appear to have no obvious and direct relationship with the ongoing thread in the story. For instance, why was Rachel able to conceive only after Leah had stopped giving birth? Was there any reason that Rachel died around the same time when Reuben defiled his father's bed, or why are these two events recorded next

Mysteries and Adventure

to each other? Was it arbitrary that the cupbearer survived, but the baker died? Why should it be a cup that was planted in Benjamin's sack? Did Jacob err when he gave Joseph the patriarchal blessing when history has shown that Judah's tribe turned out to be the most important tribe? Scholarly articles on these snippets are scarce. Indeed, a fundamental question is: What are the purposes for these snippets, if any, in relationship to the cornerstone events?

Based on the inspiration of "these are the very Scriptures that testify about me" (John 5:39), this book uses the New Testament as the guiding light to create a framework for Jacob's life under the spell of the wrestled blessing. The framework stitches together cornerstone events—the Shechem massacre, Rachel's death, Reuben's indiscretion, Judah and Tamar, Joseph's exodus, and their reunions—to indicate a coherent divine plan that has manifested throughout the Bible, especially the New Testament. Within the framework, many minuscule details in Jacob's life story fall into place, gluing together the cornerstone events and glittering with their own spiritual meanings under the spotlight of the New Testament.

In the creation of the framework, original claims and new interpretations emerge. A litmus test for the validity of the claims and interpretations is the suitability of their meanings and consistency throughout Jacob's story and the Bible. Some examples of new claims and interpretations are the embedded two clans within the twelve tribes, nuances in Joseph's two dreams to his family, the implication of the cupbearer's survival, providence in the cupbearer's forgetfulness, the necessity of Benjamin's absence in the first Egypt trip and his presence in the second, symbolism of Benjamin, and the kingdoms of Judah and Joseph.

In the end, the book encapsulates the wrestled blessing, revisits the meaning of Jacob's struggling with God and overcoming, and reflects upon true blessedness.

Now, let the adventure begin.

Tenacious Challenger

GOD CHOSE TO BLESS Jacob and have him live out the principles of blessing for all blessing chasers, as the apostle Paul wrote, "before the twins were born or had done anything good or bad—in order that God's purpose in election might stand: not by works but by him who calls—she was told, 'The older will serve the younger.' Just as it is written: 'Jacob I loved, but Esau I hated'" (Rom 9:11–13). Throughout his life, Jacob engaged in fierce battles with his adversaries, first twin brother, Esau, then uncle Laban, and at last God. In the first two-thirds of his life, up to age ninety-seven, Jacob succeeded in whatever he did. In the last third of his life, in which he struggled with God, he still won, with a profound and unexpected outcome filled with deep spiritual and prophetic implications.

In his battles, Jacob challenged the biological order by luring Esau into selling his birthright and then the ethical boundary by impersonating Esau. He challenged the odds of genetic laws by raising a large herd of streaked, speckled, or spotted animals from non-streaked, non-speckled, and non-spotted animals. He even challenged the divine protocol by taking hostage "the man" to exchange a blessing.

At the onset, Jacob fought for the finish line when he and Esau were still in Rebekah's womb. Being the firstborn in the family inherited not only a double portion of wealth but also the blessing from the patriarch.

Tenacious Challenger

The babies jostled each other within her . . . When the time came for her to give birth, there were twin boys in her womb. The first to come out was red, and his whole body was like a hairy garment; so, they named him Esau. After this, his brother came out, with his hand grasping Esau's heel. (Gen 25:22, 24–26)

Jacob came out second, but this setback in the womb did not deter him but only made him more determined in the world outside. Jacob would not accept the biological order as the deciding factor for his fortune—he challenged that tradition by making the birthright transactional. One day when Jacob was cooking some stew, Esau returned from the open country from hunting famished. He said to Jacob, "Quick, let me have some of that red stew!" Calm, calculating, and precise, Jacob asked Esau to sell his birthright, to which Esau readily agreed, "Look, I am about to lie. What good is the birthright to me?" Next, Jacob had Esau swear by it. After Esau swore, Jacob gave him some bread and the stew. Although Esau was a skillful game hunter, Jacob was an even better fortune hunter. Jacob reversed their fortune by gaining the right of the firstborn without being born first, and he did it so stealthily that Esau showed no qualms about it because "he ate and drank, and then got up and left" (Gen 25:34). Only at a later time, Esau regretted, "Isn't he rightly named Jacob? This is the second time he has taken advantage of me: He took my birthright, and now he's taken my blessing!" (Gen 27:36). By challenging the biological order, Jacob won his first battle.

Getting the birthright did not mean that Jacob would automatically get the patriarchal blessing from Isaac because Isaac loved Esau and in his old age wanted to bless Esau. Upon learning Isaac was about to bless Esau, Rebekah asked Jacob to pretend to be Esau to get the blessing. Both Jacob and Rebekah knew that they were challenging an ethical principle, as Jacob said, "I would appear to be tricking him and would bring down a curse on myself rather than a blessing." Rebekah agreed but was willing to accept the consequences. "My son, let the curse fall on me. Just do what I say; go and get them for me" (Gen 27:12–13). Isaac questioned

Jacob's voice and his quick return from hunting but was otherwise convinced by the smell of Esau's clothes that Jacob donned. By challenging ethical principles, Jacob won his second battle.

Jacob's second victory came with a cost—he had to flee from Esau, who vowed to kill Jacob when Isaac died. Jacob took refuge in Laban's house and began his solo struggle with the household. Laban cheated him by giving Leah instead of Rachel for marriage and then changed his wages ten times. To avoid being cheated again through wages, Jacob asked as wages every speckled and spotted livestock. Laban immediately put all speckled, spotted, and dark-colored livestock under his own sons' care and let Jacob start afresh with a herd with a homogeneous color. Jacob's flocks defied genetic laws and bore disproportionately many streaked or speckled or spotted young. Jacob confided to his wives,

> God has not allowed him to harm me. If he said, "The speckled ones will be your wages," then all the flocks gave birth to speckled young; and if he said, "The streaked ones will be your wages," then all the flocks bore streaked young. So God has taken away your father's livestock and has given them to me. In breeding season I once had a dream in which I looked up and saw that the male goats mating with the flock were streaked, speckled or spotted. The angel of God said to me in the dream, . . . "Look up and see that all the male goats mating with the flock are streaked, speckled or spotted, for I have seen all that Laban has been doing to you." (Gen 31:7–12)

Jacob grew exceedingly prosperous and provoked jealousy and anger from Laban's household. By challenging the odds of genetic laws, Jacob won his third battle.

Dubious Resort

NATURALLY, ONE WONDERS WHETHER Isaac's blessing attained illegitimately would lose its power. Or was Isaac's blessing, even misguided, like a contract that would work like a genie: whoever got hold of it could command it to perform at will?

On the one hand, Isaac's blessing to Jacob seemed to be binding. When Esau begged Isaac for a second blessing, Isaac replied, "I have made him lord over you and have made all his relatives his servants, and I have sustained him with grain and new wine. So what can I possibly do for you, my son?" (Gen 27:37). Further, this blessing seemed to have taken full effect for the twenty years when Jacob stayed at Laban's house. Jacob arrived as an empty-handed bachelor but left with a family—even though it had incessant quarrels—two wives, eleven sons, a daughter, and a large amount of property that provoked jealousy from Laban's family. God's blessing on Jacob was so evident that even Laban admitted that he was too blessed because of Jacob.

On the other hand, the blessing appeared not to have materialized because it fell well short of expectations. Twenty years later, Jacob fled from Laban and was about to meet Esau near Mahanaim. A messenger came to Jacob and reported that Esau led an army of four hundred waiting for Jacob at the gorge of Jabbok. At that time, Jacob had only a few dozens of family members and servants. Thus, by comparison, Esau seemed to be the blessed one. Esau's menacing presence not only frightened Jacob but also stirred up doubts about Isaac's blessing. Didn't Isaac's blessing say about getting "heaven's dew and earth's richness and be lord over his brothers"? The reality at Jabbok had a different outlook. Esau had heaven's dew and earth's richness and could trample Jacob's group anytime. This doubt about Isaac's blessing made Jacob ask for a new blessing when he wrestled with "the man." Thus, did Isaac's blessing for Jacob come to fruition or not? A detailed study of Isaac's blessing on Jacob will elucidate this question.

Blessings Misplaced

JACOB GOT HIS FIRST blessing from Isaac. When Isaac was old and his eyesight was failing, he decided to bless his firstborn, Esau, before he died. So, he called for Esau to hunt for his favorite wild game and then bless him afterward. Rebekah overheard the conversation and wanted Isaac's blessing to come to Jacob. While Esau was in the field hunting, Rebekah prepared some food the way Isaac liked, dressed Jacob in Esau's clothes, and covered his hands and neck with goatskins because Esau was hairy. Isaac was initially suspicious by Jacob's voice and how quickly he returned but was convinced, by the smell of the clothes, that it was Esau. After the hearty meal, Isaac blessed Jacob.

Did Isaac's blessing, gained by guile, materialize, especially during Jacob's stay at Laban's house after Jacob fled from the angry Esau? To answer, we first look at the contents of Isaac's blessing. Isaac said,

> Ah, the smell of my son
>   is like the smell of a field
>   that the Lord has blessed.
> May God give you heaven's dew
>   and earth's richness—
>   an abundance of grain and new wine.
> May nations serve you
>   and peoples bow down to you.

Struggle with God and Overcome

> Be lord over your brothers,
>   and may the sons of your mother bow down to you.
> May those who curse you be cursed
>   and those who bless you be blessed. (Gen 27:27–29)

The smell convinced and delighted Isaac and broke open the gate of blessing. There are two main parts to this blessing. The first is an abundance of grain and new wine, and the second, a relationship with his brothers and others. Although Jacob did not plant grain but raised livestock, "abundance of grain and new wine" meant material abundance in general. For this part, Laban and Jacob both agreed that God had blessed Jacob. Laban said to Jacob, "If I have found favor in your eyes, please stay. I have learned by divination that the Lord has blessed me because of you" (Gen 30:27). Jacob agreed, "You know how I have worked for you and how your livestock has fared under my care. The little you had before I came has increased greatly, and the Lord has blessed you wherever I have been" (Gen 30:29–30).

To further understand the nature of the blessing that Jacob received, Jacob's blessing is compared with Esau's, which came after Esau discovered he was cheated on and begged Isaac for another. For Esau, Isaac said,

> Your dwelling will be
>   away from the earth's richness,
>   away from the dew of heaven above.
> You will live by the sword
>   and you will serve your brother.
> But when you grow restless,
>   you will throw his yoke
>   from off your neck. (Gen 27:39–40)

Isaac's blessings on Jacob and Esau are both exclusive and competitive. It is exclusive because Jacob would get earth's richness and the dew of heaven, but Esau would be away from the earth's richness and the dew of heaven. This statement resembles the situation with Isaac and Ishmael, in which Isaac stayed at home, but Ishmael was ousted to the desert. Further, unlike Isaac and Ishmael, the brothers do not have their own kingdoms. When Abraham sent Hagar and Ishmael to the desert, God heard their cry and promised Hagar, "I will make him into a great nation" (Gen 21:18). In contrast, Jacob would lord over his brothers, and Esau would serve Jacob. Furthermore, their relationship is competitive. The servant brother would not submit willingly but would live by the sword and grow restless, seeking every opportunity to "throw the yoke from off his neck."

Had this blessing come to fruition, Jacob would be more prosperous and more powerful than Esau. However, at the bank of Jabbok, Jacob was astonished to see Esau's army of four hundred, outnumbering his entourage of dozens which consisted of family members and servants. He then realized that Isaac's blessing had not materialized. Regarding the second part of Isaac's blessing, let alone lording over his brother, Esau, Jacob's very life was being threatened such that he urgently arranged groups of servants crossing the river ahead of him with gifts to pacify Esau. Probably out of the realization of the "failure" of Isaac's blessing, Jacob grabbed onto God for a new blessing at the end of the wrestling match.

Isaac's Patriarchal Benediction

So, if Isaac's blessing did not materialize on Jacob, what could account for the material abundance that both Jacob and Laban acknowledged as God's blessing at Laban's house? Before Jacob left for Laban's place, Isaac gave Jacob a second blessing. In this blessing, Isaac passed God's promise to Abraham to Jacob. "So Isaac called for Jacob and blessed him . . . May God Almighty bless you and make you fruitful and increase your numbers until you become a community of peoples. May he give you and your descendants the blessing given to Abraham, so that you may take possession of the land where you now reside as a foreigner, the land God gave to Abraham" (Gen 28:1–4). God immediately affirmed this second blessing at Bethel, where Jacob laid down to rest on the way to Laban's place.

> He had a dream in which he saw a stairway resting on the earth, with its top reaching to heaven, and the angels of God were ascending and descending on it. There above it stood the Lord, and he said: "I am the Lord, the God of your father Abraham and the God of Isaac. I will give you and your descendants the land on which you are lying. Your descendants will be like the dust of the earth, and you will spread out to the west and to the east, to the north and to the south. All peoples on earth will be blessed through you and your offspring. I am with you and will watch over you wherever you go, and I will bring

you back to this land. I will not leave you until I have done what I have promised you." (Gen 28:12–15)

The key phase in God's revelation was "I am with you and will watch over you wherever you go." Because of this affirmed blessing, God's presence was evident in ensuring that Jacob would not leave Laban empty-handed and that Laban would not harm Jacob as he pursued Jacob. To keep Jacob for six more years of labor, Laban agreed to Jacob's proposed wage of getting speckled or spotted, or dark-colored lambs and goats. On the same day, Laban placed all such mixed-color lambs and goats in the care of his sons and put a three-day journey between himself and Jacob. Therefore, to earn his wage, Jacob would have to produce mixed-color animals from the solid-color animals, namely, the existing non-speckled, non-spotted, and non-dark-colored livestock. For this to happen, it would require supernatural intervention, and God did just that. An angel of God said to Jacob in a dream, "Look up and see that all the male goats mating with the flock are streaked, speckled or spotted, for I have seen all that Laban has been doing to you" (Gen 31:12). This act from God made Jacob's flock grow exceedingly prosperous.

God's promise to be with Jacob also manifested in protection when Laban decided to pursue Jacob. God appeared to him and warned him of harming Jacob (Gen 31:29). To assure Jacob of the origin of these benefits, the angel of God made the clear identification that "I am the God of Bethel, where you anointed a pillar and where you made a vow to me" (Gen 31:13). This statement unequivocally declares that Isaac's second blessing brought Jacob abundance and protection.

Then, did Isaac's first blessing simply vanish? Absolutely not. Its consequence and resolution played out at the gorge of Jabbok, as discussed in the next chapter.

Gorge of Jabbok

ARRIVING AT THE RIVERBANK of Jabbok was a watershed moment in Jacob's life. He must confront his past at the human level and the spiritual level. At the human level, he faced the consequences of stealing Isaac's blessing from Esau. At the spiritual level, he faced the benevolence and judgment of God, who, on the one hand, promised to protect and bless him and, on the other hand, would not tolerate blemishes in the dealing of his blessings. The camps from the three parties all converged at Mahanaim: Jacob's entire family, Esau's four hundred strong army, and God's angels (Gen 32:1–2).

The resolution at the spiritual level took place before the human level. At night, a man came to wrestle with Jacob, and the match had to end before daybreak.

> So Jacob was left alone, and a man wrestled with him till daybreak.
>
> When the man saw that he could not overpower him, he touched the socket of Jacob's hip so that his hip was wrenched as he wrestled with the man.
>
> Then the man said, "Let me go, for it is daybreak."
>
> But Jacob replied, "I will not let you go unless you bless me."
>
> The man asked him, "What is your name?"
>
> "Jacob," he answered.
>
> Then the man said, "Your name will no longer be Jacob, but Israel, because you have struggled with God and with humans and have overcome."

Gorge of Jabbok

Jacob said, "Please tell me your name."

But he replied, "Why do you ask my name?" Then he blessed him there.

So Jacob called the place Peniel, saying, "It is because I saw God face to face, and yet my life was spared."

The sun rose above him as he passed Peniel, and he was limping because of his hip. (Gen 32:24–31)

Mysteries surrounded this encounter. Was the wrestling real, as opposed to Jacob's inner struggle with his alter ego? Who was "the man"? Why did Jacob wrestle with a stranger all night? During the day, Jacob prayed for God's protection, but by night, why did he plead for blessing rather than protection? Why did "the man" declare that Jacob won the match even though he had the power to cripple Jacob by merely touching him?

Some scholars proposed that "the man" was Jacob's own inner being or alter ego wrestling with itself. However, the crippling injury to Jacob showed that it was an actual physical contest. Then, who was "the man" and why did he come? Upon knowing Esau's army of four hundred in wait, Jacob appealed to God the Bethel promise that would save him and his family from Esau (Gen 32:9–12). It was probable that "the man" came in response to his prayer. In Old Testament times, visitors from above arrived when significant events were imminent. When Sodom and Gomorrah were to be destroyed, three men visited Abraham to alert him of the event: "Shall I hide from Abraham what I am about to do?" (Gen 18:17). Similarly, two angels arrived at Sodom to rescue Lot and his family the night before Sodom and Gomorrah were destroyed. The night at Jabbok was on the verge of such a significant event: Esau's force could wipe out Jacob's whole family. Jacob already sensed the presence of angels of God in the surroundings and called the place Mahanaim, "the camp of God" (Gen 32:1–2). Therefore, the appearance of the man should not surprise him. The man came as Jacob probably anticipated, and Jacob recognized and engaged with the visitor till daybreak.

However, unlike Abraham's and Lot's situation, instead of providing hospitality, Jacob wrestled with him. Why? Wrestling indicated contention over an issue, which in context could be reconciliation with Esau. Jacob had planned well for the meeting by pacifying Esau with gifts, breaking his caravan into groups, each of which was loaded with livestock gifts, and parading them ahead of himself.

> He [Jacob] spent the night there, and from what he had with him he selected a gift for his brother Esau: two hundred female goats and twenty male goats, two hundred ewes and twenty rams, thirty female camels with their young, forty cows and ten bulls, and twenty female donkeys and ten male donkeys. He put them in the care of his servants, each herd by itself, and said to his servants, "Go ahead of me, and keep some space between the herds."
>
> He instructed the one in the lead: "When my brother Esau meets you and asks, 'Who do you belong to, and where are you going, and who owns all these animals in front of you?' then you are to say, 'They belong to your servant Jacob. They are a gift sent to my lord Esau, and he is coming behind us.'"
>
> He also instructed the second, the third and all the others who followed the herds: "You are to say the same thing to Esau when you meet him. And be sure to say, 'Your servant Jacob is coming behind us.'" For he thought, "I will pacify him with these gifts I am sending on ahead; later, when I see him, perhaps he will receive me." So Jacob's gifts went on ahead of him, but he himself spent the night in the camp. (Gen 32:13–21)

Although the Bible did not disclose the message from the visitor, we can infer it from the complete reversal of Jacob's behavior the next morning. On the next day's morning, instead of hiding behind the parade of gifts and family as originally planned, he walked in front of the groups, bowing down to the ground seven times as he approached his brother, contrary to Isaac's first blessing that "the sons of your mother bow down to you." Because the only influence on Jacob during the night was the visitor, this new plan must have come from him. The new plan was to admit his past wrongs and humble himself. The seven bows meant completeness and connoted origination from God. While the original plan had the colors of a human approach, the new plan had a distinct divine flavor—humility and repentance. Jacob and the man tussled over the plans of reconciliation.

In view of the menace of Esau's army, Isaac's first blessing appeared to have failed. This new reconciliation plan now seemed to put the icing on the cake by explicitly nullifying Isaac's blessing that "the sons of your mother bow down to you." Jacob sought a replacement and thus held on to the man for a new blessing.

If Jacob abandoned his own and accepted the new plan, why did "the man" declare that Jacob won, "because you have struggled with God and with humans and have overcome" (Gen 32:28)? Didn't God win by making Jacob follow the new plan? Even more perplexing was that "the man" had the power to cripple Jacob by merely touching him but would not overcome Jacob. Why did Jacob win? On the surface level, the competitor would lose by default if he had to leave, and "the man" wanted to leave before daybreak so that Jacob's life would be spared as he saw God face to face (Gen 32:30). On the spiritual level, the context was about getting blessings. Against humans, Jacob won the match of blessing grabbing from Esau and Laban; by the same token, Jacob won the blessing from his wrestling opponent. A deeper answer to this question is relegated to the end of the book.

Watershed Moment

THE FACE-TO-FACE ENCOUNTER WITH God was the watershed moment in Jacob's life and was marked by three significant overnight changes in Jacob: body, mind, and life.

First, Jacob's body has changed—permanently crippled. Jacob was no brawn like Esau and preferred stewing lentil soup to hunting; nevertheless, he was a skillful and strong wrestler such that the man at Jabbok could not overpower him at the human level. However, a supernatural touch made him weak. Some commentators view the hip injury as a punishment for Jacob's sin against Esau. A problem with this view is that the type of punishment does not fit the nature of the crime. Further, Esau later forgave Jacob; so, physical punishment should not be called for. The hip injury was imparted to commemorate the encounter with God and to end permanently Jacob's future struggle, or wrestling, for blessings. The wrestling with God has given him the ultimate blessing.

Second, Jacob's mind has changed. Before the wrestling match, Jacob never changed his mind, and setbacks only strengthened his determination. When cheated by Laban into marrying Leah, Jacob was deterred but simply worked for another seven years to marry Rachel. When Laban changed Jacob's wages ten times, Jacob stayed steadfast. When the man wanted to leave at daybreak, Jacob wouldn't let go unless he blessed Jacob. To change a person's mind, the person's worldview must first be changed.

WATERSHED MOMENT

Jacob's worldview had been groomed from his experiences. In his worldview, a blessing was all about materials, and he was the master orchestrating wealth accumulation, with God as a "servant" who produced in need and protected in danger. When Jacob faced the hard problem of producing mixed-color animals from solid-color animals, God produced the miracle of the birth of speckled, streaked, and spotted lambs and kids. When Jacob's life was endangered, God warned Laban. To face Esau, Jacob resorted to a plan based on his worldview: on the one hand, pacify Esau with gifts; on the other hand, pray God would protect him if Esau would not abide. However, this time God had a different idea. God wanted Jacob to first mend the relationship with Esau by humbling himself. Jacob wrestled with the suggestion all night but eventually yielded, abandoning his material-driven scheme for God's humbling approach. Jacob took up the challenge with faith, knowing full well the danger of walking in the front of the group to the eruption point of suppressed hatred of twenty years.

By faith, Jacob changed from a coward, who would hide behind the livestock and his family, believing materials would instantly heal the wound that lasted for twenty years, to a courageous leader who walked ahead of the family and humbled himself seven times, in sharp contrast to Isaac's blessing that "the sons of your mother bow down to you." The humility led to a miraculous change of heart in Esau as he ran to meet Jacob and embraced him; he threw his arms around his neck and kissed him. When Jacob offered the gifts, Esau declined: "I already have plenty, my brother. Keep what you have for yourself" (Gen 33:9). Through faith, Jacob witnessed how God turned Esau's hostility into love and forgiveness. This miracle shattered Jacob's materialistic worldview: humility, not materials, brought forth reconciliation and peace and kindled a spiritual awakening: yielding to God's will by faith is a true blessing.

Finally, Jacob's name has changed. At daybreak, the man said to Jacob, "Your name will no longer be Jacob, but Israel, because you have struggled with God and with humans and have overcome" (Gen 32:28). In Old Testament times, a name change often indicated a change in life. When God pronounced to Abraham and Sarah that they would be father and mother of nations, God changed their names as a witness to the covenant. At that time, Abraham was ninety-nine years old, and thus the name change was a seal of certainty of the promise. Jacob's change of worldview inevitably led to a change in his life and thus his name. As the name "Israel" (meaning "struggle with God") implies, the rest of Jacob's life will be a struggle with God, and the spark of faith that Jacob showed as he headed to Esau heralds what Jacob would need to cope with the struggle.

The three changes in Jacob—body, mind, and life—ushered in a period of upheaval in Jacob's life where only the faithful could survive. This period centered around the blessing bestowed at the daybreak. Unlike the case with Abraham, God did not initiate the blessing, but Jacob "wrestled" it from God, or he would not let the man leave. Further, the contents of Jacob's wrestled blessing were not revealed in the Bible. Could this blessing be similar to the one that Jacob received at Bethel, but its contents were omitted for brevity? Or could this blessing be something mundane that the Bible did not record, and it had nothing to do with the tragic events in the rest of Jacob's life because these events defy the definition of blessing? Or was this blessing remarkedly different and so significant that it called for a name change on the recipient? Since this blessing was pronounced on Jacob, it should have manifested in Jacob's lifetime. A detailed study of Jacob's life thereafter is therefore warranted.

Life Stages

BEFORE A DETAILED EXAMINATION of Jacob's life after the blessing from the wrestling match, it is helpful to get an overview of his life and the key milestones to establish a perspective for later analyses.

After Jacob deceived Isaac for the blessing intended for Esau, Jacob left home in Beersheba and traveled northeast to his uncle Laban's home in Harran, starting his exile in Canaan at the age of seventy-seven. On the way, Jacob had a dream in Bethel, in which God appeared to Jacob for the first time and promised to give the land to Jacob and bring him back (Gen 28:13–15).

Jacob spent twenty years at Laban's house. To marry Laban's daughter Rachel, Jacob worked for seven years. However, on the wedding night, Laban gave his eldest daughter, Leah, instead, citing the custom that an older daughter had to marry before a younger one. For Rachel, Jacob worked for another seven years. At the end of the fourteen years, Joseph, Rachel's first son, was born. Laban saw in his prosperity God's hand because of Jacob and asked Jacob to stay longer. After six years, Jacob's property grew so much that it incurred jealousy from Laban's family; so, Jacob packed and quietly left Harran, returning home. Laban chased and caught up with Jacob's convoy in the hill country of Gilead, but the two made a pact and separated peacefully. At this time, Jacob was ninety-seven years old.

At the same time, Esau and an army of four hundred came from Seir to meet Jacob. Before crossing the ford of the Jabbok,

Struggle with God and Overcome

Jacob divided the convoy into groups carrying gifts and sent them ahead of himself. At night, Jacob wrestled with God at Peniel. The next morning, Jacob and Esau met and reconciled.

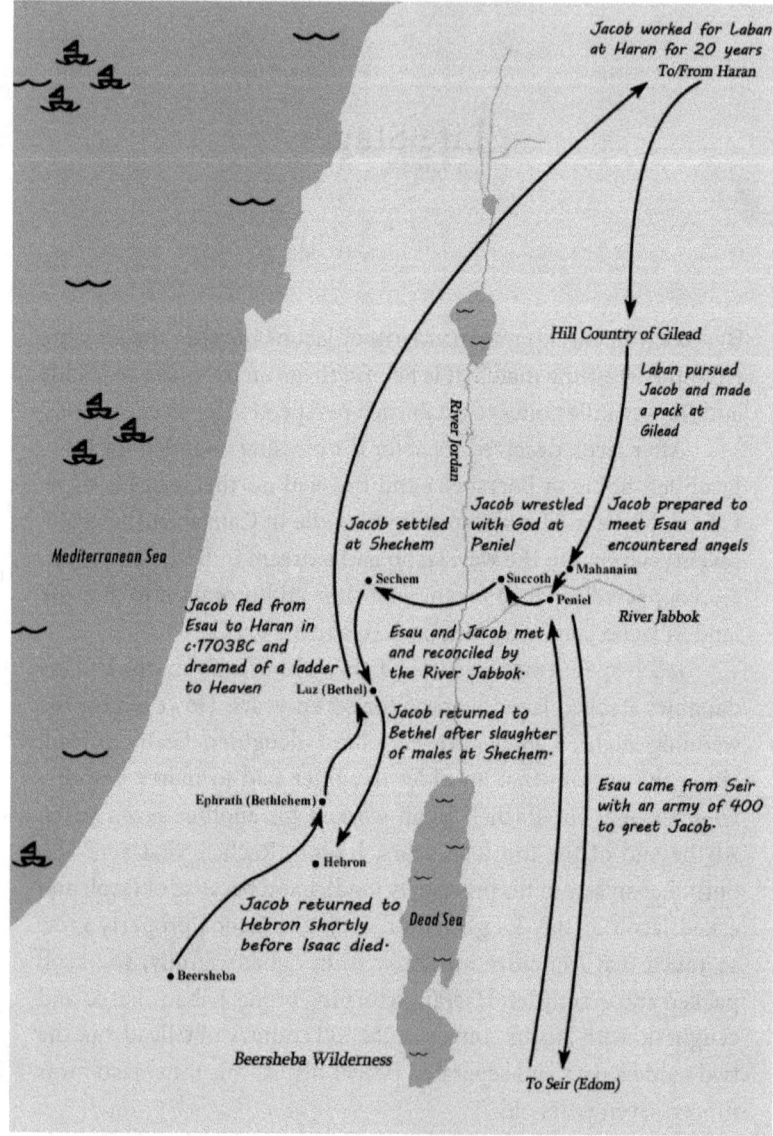

Figure 1. Jacob's exile

Life Stages

Jacob proceeded to settle at Shechem for some years. After Simeon and Levi killed the men in Shechem and plundered the city, Jacob moved again, back to Bethel, where God appeared to Jacob again, reiterating the blessing of Abraham and Isaac and Jacob's name change to Israel. God's appearance marked the end of Jacob's exile and signified a new era in Jacob's life (Gen 35:9–13). Figure 1 shows Jacob's exile routes and the related events.

Around this time, Rachel died while giving birth to Benjamin, and Reuben slept with Jacob's concubine Bilhah. These two incidents stopped Jacob from having more children and thus completed the formation of the twelve tribes. Immediately after these two incidents, the Bible summarizes the twelve sons of Jacob (Gen 35:19–26).

The rest of Jacob's life centers around Joseph. Joseph was six years old when Jacob left Laban and was seventeen when he was sold to Egypt. So, Joseph went missing eleven years after Jacob left Laban. Thus Jacob was one hundred eight years old when Joseph was missing, calculated by adding eleven to Jacob's age of ninety-seven at the time he departed from Laban. Joseph became Egypt's governor at the age of thirty and reunited with his brothers after seven years of harvest and two years of famine. Jacob entered Egypt at one hundred thirty and died at one hundred forty-seven. A timeline of Jacob's life is shown in Fig. 2.

Based on the above timeline, Jacob's life has four stages. Stage 1 is from his birth to the wrestling match in Jabbok and spans ninety-seven years. In this period, Jacob was the master of his life, having struggled with humans and overcome, as "the man" at the wrestling said, first with Esau and then Laban. Stage 2, eleven years, ends when Joseph was sold to Egypt; and stage 3, twenty-two years, concludes when Jacob was reunited with Joseph in Egypt. The thirty-three years following the wrestling match, the combination of stages 2 and 3, is the time struggling with God—as iconized by his new name, Israel—that manifests the wrestled blessing and is the jewel of Jacob's spiritual journey. It will be clear later that this period of thirty-three years should be divided into two stages. These thirty-three years will be called Jacob's mission years. The final stage, the seventeen years that Jacob lived in Egypt till his death, is the capstone of his blessed life.

Struggle with God and Overcome

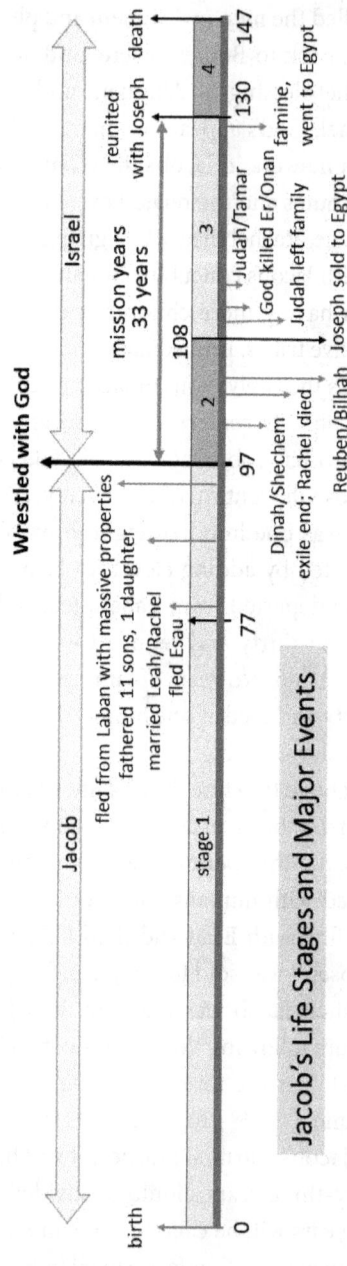

Figure 2. Jacob's life timeline

Turn of Events

OF ALL THE EVENTS in his life, Jacob's wrestle with God at Jabbok stood out as the most significant turning point in his life. He changed overnight, from hiding behind the parade of gifts, servants, and family members to leading the way to reconciliation with Esau. Afterward, his life would change so much that God told him that his name would be called Israel. Furthermore, his "fortune" also took an unexpected turn.

Throughout his first stage of life, Jacob had a smooth life: things worked out the way he planned, for example, trading stew for Esau's birthright, receiving Esau's blessing, and amassing a large amount of livestock from Laban. The only tense moments were direct consequences of Jacob's own undertaking, for instance, fleeing from Esau and Laban. No one was physically harmed and no lives were lost in this period.

Since wrestling with God, Jacob experienced quite the opposite during the following thirty-three years: nightmares seemed to follow him wherever he went. In Shechem, his only daughter, Dinah, was defiled. To revenge for their sister, Simeon and Levi tricked the men in the city to be circumcised and then slaughtered them and plundered the city, a crime that forced Jacob's family to flee to Bethel. During the journey, his beloved wife Rachel died upon giving birth to Benjamin. While Jacob was away, his eldest son, Reuben, slept with Jacob's concubine Bilhah. Next, his favorite son, Joseph, disappeared, presumably torn apart by wild animals. At about the same time, two of his grandsons, Er and Onan, were struck down by God. Furthermore, famine came and threatened the livelihood of the whole family. During this period, there was nothing but bad news for Jacob. This drastic change in Jacob's life was foretold when God asked Jacob to change his name to Israel because, in biblical times, a name often reflected a person's life or character. For example, God changed Abram's name to Abraham to mark God's promise to make him a father of many nations (Gen 17:5–7).

It might be tempting to interpret these troubles as consequences of sin or judgments from God on, for instance, Jacob's deception on Isaac and Esau. However, they happened after the relationship with Esau was restored and Jacob received a new blessing. Even more perplexing is that, during the hardship in Canaan, God had been with Jacob all along and seemed to allow these events to happen. God told Jacob to return to Bethel after Simeon and Levi slaughtered all males in the city and caused terror to fall on the towns all around them so that no one pursued them (Gen 35:1, 5). If God wanted to exact justice from Jacob in Shechem, God would simply allow the indigenous people to pursue them. Upon settling in Bethel, God again appeared to Jacob and reiterated the blessing of Abraham and Isaac (Gen 35:11–12). Then for the next thirty years or so, God was quiet and only spoke to Jacob again when Jacob set foot to meet Joseph in Egypt. That is, God did not give any warnings about his impending judgment but only blessings. Therefore, the troubles in these thirty-three years were not judgments from God on the family's sins.

What a turn of fate! What could have caused all these difficulties? The only major event preceding this fateful time is the wrestling match, and hence the mystery must lie within it. The blessing at the end of the match has several distinctive traits. First, God did not initiate the blessing. Instead, Jacob insisted on a blessing or would not let the man leave. Second, the Bible does not disclose the contents of the blessing; it is unusual because the Bible reveals the contents of all other blessings on Jacob. Finally, this blessing is so significant that it called for a change of Jacob's name. If this wrestled blessing indeed leads to these events, what spiritual messages do these adversities carry? Further, "the man" remarked that "you have struggled with God and humans and have overcome." Could this fateful time be an actual struggle with God as the name Israel suggests? But then, what does it mean to "struggle with God and have overcome"? All these set the stage for a thorough investigative study.

Methodology

TO EXPLORE THE SPIRITUAL meanings of the events in Jacob's life following the wrestling, we will examine each of the events in Jacob's life stages 2 and 3, which are recorded in Genesis chapters 34–35 and 37–45. These events include the incident at Shechem, Rachel's death and Reuben's indiscretion, Judah and Tamar, Joseph's abduction, his imprisonment, dream interpretations, rise in Egypt, and the reunion of the brothers with Joseph in Egypt.

These events are recorded in chronological order, except for the story of Judah and Tamar, which occurs at about the same time as Joseph's departure for Egypt. Thus, our exploration will follow the sequence in the Bible.

For each event, we extract the representative elements to construct a summary. The message and meaning in each summary are then interpreted in the light of the Bible, especially the New Testament. Based on the similarities of encounters and actions of the characters in the events, we identify the characters' counterparts in the New Testament and henceforth infer parallels between the characters in Jacob's story and those in the New Testament. This pairing of the New Testament characters with those in Jacob's story must be consistent with all the episodes in the life of Jacob and the messages in the New Testament.

These summaries are pericopes of God's overall plan in Jacob's mission years. Next, these pericopes, like the pieces in a jigsaw puzzle, along with the New Testament parallels, are pieced together

METHODOLOGY

to form an overall picture. From the overall picture, we deduce the spiritual meanings in the thirty-three years of Jacob's life and come to conclude the blessing that Jacob wrestled from God.

Shechem

IN THE FIRST STAGE of Jacob's life, God promised him in Bethel of Abraham's and Isaac's promise that "I will give you and your descendants the land on which you are lying. Your descendants will be like the dust of the earth, and you will spread out to the west and to the east, to the north and to the south. All peoples on earth will be blessed through you and your offspring." Furthermore, God also added that "I am with you and will watch over you wherever you go, and I will bring you back to this land. I will not leave you until I have done what I have promised you" (Gen 28:13–15).

In this stage of his life, the manifestation of this blessing embodies what a blessing is commonly understood, namely worldview prosperity. Regarding progeny, Jacob had eleven sons and one daughter in the twenty years at Laban's house. When it came to wealth, God made Jacob's livestock grow more than Laban's. When Laban decided to chase Jacob down, God warned Laban about it. This span of his life can be best summarized as Jacob struggling with men and having overcome.

As prophesized in the wrestling match, Jacob's later life did not struggle with men but with God. Thus, the ensuing investigation examines the events in Jacob's second and third stages from God's perspective, interpreting the events under God's purposes and plans. For example, how an incident serves to embody a message about the elected people.

Shechem

The first event in Jacob's second life stage happened in the city of Shechem in Canaan, where Jacob bought a parcel of land from the sons of Hamor, the father of Shechem. Jacob's only daughter, Dinah, went out to visit the women of the land and was raped by Shechem, the son of Hamor the Hivite. Dinah's brothers were shocked and furious. Shechem loved Dinah and wanted to marry her. Shechem's father, Hamor, then talked to Jacob and her brothers about the marriage and offered to give whatever they asked.

> Jacob's sons replied deceitfully as they spoke to Shechem and his father Hamor. They said to them, "We can't do such a thing; we can't give our sister to a man who is not circumcised. That would be a disgrace to us. We will enter into an agreement with you on one condition only: that you become like us by circumcising all your males. Then we will give you our daughters and take your daughters for ourselves."

Their proposal seemed good to Hamor and his son Shechem, who then spoke to the men of the city. "Won't their livestock, their property and all their other animals become ours?" (Gen 34:23). So, all the men of the city agreed and were circumcised. So, the men of the city had in their mind material gains when they accepted circumcision.

> Three days later, while all of them were still in pain, two of Jacob's sons, Simeon and Levi, Dinah's brothers, took their swords and attacked the unsuspecting city, killing every male . . . They seized their flocks and herds and donkeys and everything else of theirs in the city and out in the fields. They carried off all their wealth and all their women and children, taking as plunder everything in the houses.

Now the two sons of Jacob demonstrated the family tradition of trickery, but only to a more extreme extent. They killed not only the perpetrator but also all the men in the city. Even in the law of the Old Testament, the death penalty is not commensurate to the crime of rape. In Deuteronomy, the law states that "if a man happens to meet a virgin who is not pledged to be married and rapes her and they are discovered, he shall pay her father fifty shekels of silver. He must marry the young woman, for he has violated her. He can never divorce her as long as he lives" (Deut 22:28-29). Moreover, the sons took possession of Shechemites' properties. Jacob resent their actions and condemned the two brothers in his final benediction.

The atrocity of this magnitude no doubt caused intense hatred and called for revenge. God told Jacob to leave Shechem in this dangerous situation and go to Bethel, where God appeared to Jacob when he fled from Esau.

> So Jacob said to his household and to all who were with him, "Get rid of the foreign gods you have with you, and purify yourselves and change your clothes. Then come, let us go up to Bethel, where I will build an altar to God, who answered me in the day of my distress and who has been with me wherever I have gone." So they gave Jacob all the foreign gods they had and the rings in their ears, and Jacob buried them under the oak at Shechem. Then they set out, and the terror of God fell on the towns all around them so that no one pursued them. (Gen 35:2-5)

This incident was a test for Jacob's family to confront a dilemma loaded with moral, spiritual, and economic implications. Shechem made the first moral mistake. If Jacob accepted the marriage proposal, he would violate the spiritual mandate of marriage within the elected. Initially, the problem was moral but immediately developed into an economic battle, as the Shechemites realized, "Won't their livestock, their property and all their other animals become ours?" Simeon and Levi responded by breaking all moral and spiritual boundaries, trampling the sacred practice of circumcision meant for the elected, deceiving the men into circumcision, massacring them while they were still in pain, and plundering the village. The family gained economically but bankrupted morally and spiritually.

On the surface, the story is about an overzealous execution of justice in a dispute. But in essence, it is a spiritual declaration: how God's chosen people would stand out among the gentiles. On the one hand, the story tells about God and his mandates for his

SHECHEM

elected: the sacrament of circumcision, the threat of intermarriage, God's protection, and the abandonment of idols. On the other hand, it shows the failure of the elected to be exemplary for others: deception, trampling of sacrament, violence, and greed. In this test, God stood on the sideline, allowing the incident to unfold to the end, and protected the family from the indigenous people when Simeon and Levi's revenge went exceedingly cruel and unjust. The outcome of this test was a testimonial to the failure of the elected people to live out as God's chosen people, exemplifying in obeying God's mandates and moral code.

Because this event captures all the critical traits or issues characteristic of the nation of Israelites—namely, election, circumcision, providence, idols, preservation of the elected amid the threat of intermarriage, and the failure of the elected to be exemplary among gentiles—the Shechem story is a microcosm of the spiritual condition of the nation of Israelites in the Old Testament time. If Jacob's thirty-three years constitute an overall plan from God, the Shechem incident delivers the first message: the failure of the elected to be exemplary.

The first piece of the puzzle in Jacob's mission year is shown in figure 3.

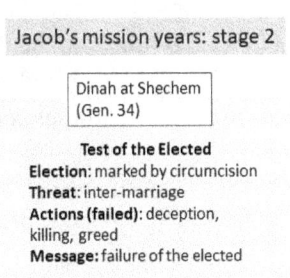

Figure 3. Test of the elected

Rachel and Reuben

UPON ARRIVAL IN BETHEL, God appeared to Jacob again, fulfilling God's promise to bring Jacob back to Bethel and marking the end of Jacob's exile. Further, God reiterated the patriarchal commitment to Jacob that God gave to Abraham and Isaac. In the end, God named him Israel. All these signify the passing of the sacred responsibility from Isaac to Jacob.

As the family moved away from Shechem, Rachel began to give birth but had great difficulty. Right after Benjamin was born, Rachel died and was buried near Bethlehem. Around the same time, Reuben slept with Jacob's concubine Bilhah, Rachel's maid, and Jacob learned of it. At this junction, the Bible lists the twelve sons of Jacob, hinting that Rachel's death and Reuben's action have ended future children from Jacob and thus completed the formation of the tribes.

Leah and her servant Zilpah stopped childbearing since Leah gave birth to their only daughter, Dinah. Reuben's indiscretion made Jacob spurn Bilhah. Therefore, with Rachel's death, there were no more children for Jacob, thus completing Jacob's family, the twelve sons. The first ten sons were born of Leah, Zilpah, and Bilhah. Then, daughter Dinah came. Finally, Rachel gave birth to Joseph and Benjamin. Dinah delineates the twelve sons into two groups, the first ten sons in one group and the last two in another. This topic will be explored more later.

Rachel and Reuben

Next, Isaac died at the age of a hundred eighty years. Now, Abraham and Isaac's lineage focuses solely upon Jacob. Signified by the divinely inspired name change to Israel, Jacob began the most extraordinary adventure and struggle with God in his life.

The three temporally related events—Rachel's, Reuben's discretion, and Isaac's death, mark the beginning of a new era for the nation of Israel and form the second piece of the puzzle of Jacob's mission years, shown in figure 4.

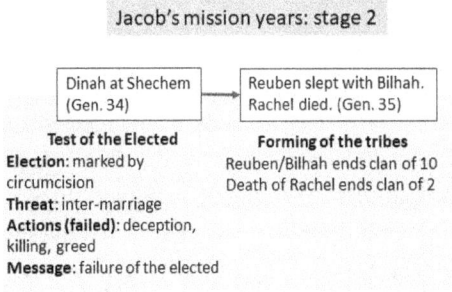

Figure 4. Forming of the tribes

Leaving the Brothers

IN JACOB'S THIRD LIFE stage, starting from Genesis chapter 37, two protagonists emerged, Joseph and Judah, who lived out their own lives separately until they reunited in Egypt. To understand the spiritual meanings of their lives, we analyze first the stories of Judah and Joseph for their symbolism in the light of God's overall plan in the Bible and then the significance of the two reunions in Egypt.

Genesis chapter 37 and from chapter 39 on are about Joseph. Thus, chapter 38 about Judah and Tamar seems out of place, as many commentators have pointed out. The sequence of telling the story about Judah, after Joseph's story has started, suggests that Judah's role in the selling of Joseph contributes to Judah's departure from the other brothers. Further, Joseph's and Judah's departures from the brothers are almost simultaneous, as indicated in the Bible. "*At that time*, Judah left his brothers and went down to stay with a man of Adullam named Hirah" (Gen 38:1). Therefore, at the expense of continuity, intertwining Judah's story with Joseph's emphasizes the simultaneity of the two separations. Thus, Judah's and Joseph's stories start on the common theme—separation from the brothers: Joseph sold to Egypt, and Judah left his brothers for Canaan.

The simultaneous breakups from the other brothers indicate the emergence of two clans, where Judah is the head of one clan, Joseph, the other. The two clans live their respective lives separately until they reunite in Egypt. The two clans signify two nations to come in the future and their stories, rich in spiritual symbolism, prophesize about the nations in the world and what to become of the world. The stories of Judah and Joseph are at the core of Jacob's thirty-three-year journey that forms the framework of manifesting God's plan for humanity consisting of two nations of God's people who will come together at the apocalypse.

Figure 5 summarizes the messages from Jacob's life second stage and the breakups of Judah and Joseph from other brothers.

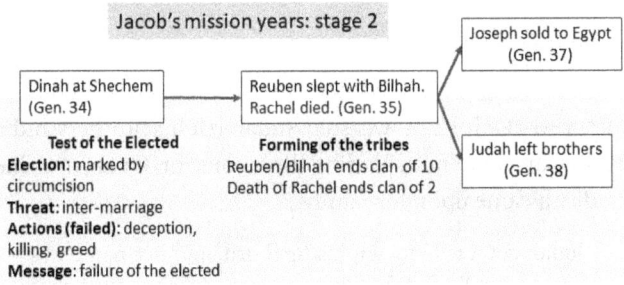

Figure 5. Jacob's life second stage

Judah and Tamar

SHORTLY AFTER JOSEPH WAS sold, Judah left his brothers and went down to Canaan to marry, siring three sons, Er, Onan, and Shelah. Then death came upon his family.

> Judah got a wife for Er, his firstborn, and her name was Tamar. But Er, Judah's firstborn, was wicked in the Lord's sight; so the Lord put him to death.
> Then Judah said to Onan, "Sleep with your brother's wife and fulfill your duty to her as a brother-in-law to raise up offspring for your brother." But Onan knew that the child would not be his; so whenever he slept with his brother's wife, he spilled his semen on the ground to keep from providing offspring for his brother. What he did was wicked in the Lord's sight; so the Lord put him to death also. (Gen 38:6–10)

Judah was afraid that his third son, Shelah, could also die had Judah asked Tamar to continue to fulfill the duty with Shelah. It appeared that Tamar was a "black widow." Using the excuse that Shelah was still too young, Judah asked Tamar to go away to live in her father's household. In fact, Judah admitted later that he had no intention to give her to Shelah.

After a long time, Judah's wife died, and Judah went up to Timnah to shear his sheep. Upon hearing this, Tamar disguised herself with a veil and sat down at the entrance to Timnah. When Judah saw her and thought she was a prostitute, he spent a night with her,

Judah and Tamar

promising to send her a young goat. As a pledge, Tamar asked for Judah's seal and its cord and his staff and disappeared from the street.

Three months later, Judah heard that his daughter-in-law was pregnant. Suspecting Tamar of prostitution, Judah said to bring her out to be burned to death. To this, she sent a message to her father-in-law. "I am pregnant by the man who owns these. See if you recognize whose seal and cord and staff these are." Judah recognized them and said, "She is more righteous than I, since I wouldn't give her to my son Shelah" (Gen 38:26).

The story ended when Tamar gave birth to two twin boys.

This was an extraordinary event in Jacob's and Judah's life. First, never before did God kill a member of the family. On the contrary, God had been their protector, not even in Shechem when Simeon and Levi murdered all the men in the city. Second, wickedness was first mentioned in the family, and judgment came swift. Finally, righteousness was also mentioned for the first time in the family.

Why is Er wicked? Is spilling semen on the ground enough for Onan to die? Why is Tamar righteous after Judah learned that he and Tamar committed incest? What is the message of this story? The Bible does not give direct answers, but we can infer them from the theme of the chapter.

What is the theme of the story? The chapter starts with the birth of Judah's three sons. The eldest son, Er, died childless. The second son, Onan, died when he refused to fulfill his duty to Er. Tamar was sent away for fear of causing Shelah death. Tamar disguised herself as a prostitute, and Judah impregnated her. Finally, two twin boys were born. Birth is the keyword, and thus the theme is about extending the family's lineage to fulfill God's promise of "be fruitful and increase in number." This promise of "be fruitful and increase in number" had been the patriarchal benediction from God since Abraham and Isaac and was passed down to Jacob. God spoke this promise twice to Jacob at Bethel, at the beginning and the end of his exile.

At that time, there was no given law; God's words were the law. Moreover, God's words were "be fruitful and increase in number," the promise of progeny. Whoever acted against or with that promise would be judged wicked or righteous. As a result, the second son, Onan, who did not want to impregnate Tamar by spilling his semen on the ground, was judged wicked. Similarly, Tamar risked her reputation and managed to extend the family's lineage, and she was called righteous. By the same token, Judah called himself not righteous for "not giving her his son Shelah." Therefore, it can be inferred that Er was wicked because he did not want to father children. The story concluded the theme with the fruition of righteousness, fulfillment of the promise: the birth of twin boys, Zerah and Perez.

God seemed harsh in this story, killing two men who might not understand the severe consequences of their actions. The story ends with an outcome of righteousness. Judah's unexpected twin boys, Zerah and Perez, replaced his two lost sons. This story demonstrated the supremacy of God's words and the balance of justice and mercy.

What is the spiritual pericope for this story? It introduced the system of justice, where the words of God were the basis upon which judgment would be rendered, wicked or righteous. This seminal system of justice was the reality that foreshadowed the laws for the nation of Israel.

Add this story's spiritual pericope to Jacob's life diagram as follows:

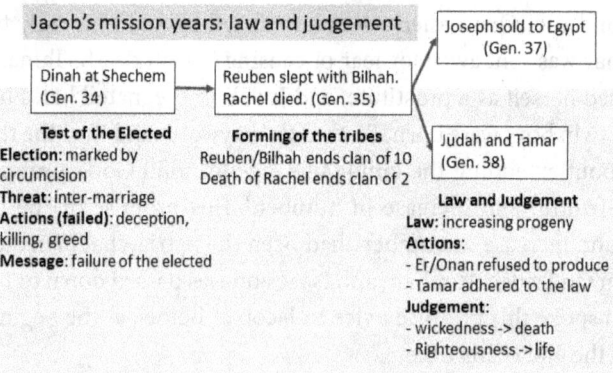

Figure 6. Bifurcation of family clans

Two Clans

DURING THE SECOND AND third stages of Jacob's life, the twelve sons of Jacob evolved into two clans, which developed into two kingdoms that would eventually merge at the end of the world. A significance of this hypothesis is that the story of Jacob is not only historical but prophetic and thus calls for further study in the light of other books in the Bible, especially the New Testament. To support this hypothesis, we analyze common traits among the brothers within each clan.

The twelves sons were born in two separate intervals. In the first interval, the ten sons of Leah, Bilhah, and Zilpah were born together. Then daughter Dinah came. After Dinah, Rachel gave birth to Joseph and Benjamin. The division suggests two groupings: the first group consists of the first ten sons, and the second group, Joseph and Benjamin. See figure 7.

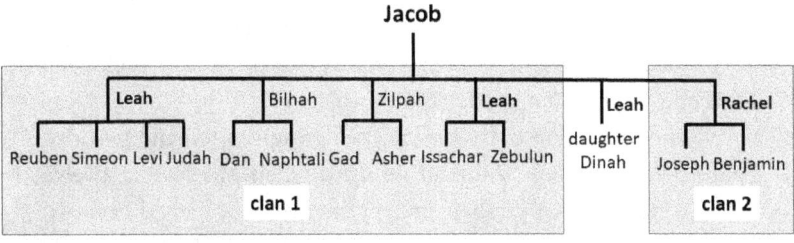

Figure 7. Jacob's family tree

Struggle with God and Overcome

Further, there is a common thread among the sons in each group. In the first group, the three women had no difficulties conceiving and giving birth. On the contrary, Rachel prayed and waited for many years before conceiving Joseph.

> Then God remembered Rachel; he listened to her and enabled her to conceive. She became pregnant and gave birth to a son and said, "God has taken away my disgrace." She named him Joseph, and said, "May the Lord add to me another son." (Gen 30:22-24)

When it came to Benjamin, Rachel died from his birth. Rachel's difficulty in childbearing was not new. It happened to the first wives of Abraham and Isaac, Sarah and Rebekah. Even though God promised Abraham and Isaac that their offspring would be like the stars in the sky, both Sarah and Rebekah had difficulty conceiving. Abraham waited until he was one hundred years old to have Isaac. Similarly, Isaac did not have a child until he "prayed to the Lord on behalf of his wife, because she was childless. The Lord answered his prayer, and his wife Rebekah became pregnant" (Gen 25:21). Because the firstborns of Abraham and Isaac came as a result of their earnest prayers and faithful wait, God's participation in the births was apparent. In this aspect, the thread—God played a central role in their progeny—runs through Abraham, Isaac, and now Jacob, Rachel, and their sons Joseph and Benjamin.

The number ten has a specific meaning in the Bible, often designating a complete representation of an entire group. For example, God brought ten plagues on Egypt (Exod 7:14—12:30); there were ten commandments; Jesus healed ten lepers (Luke 17:11-19); and Jesus talked about ten virgins (Matt 25:1-13), ten coins (Luke 15:8-10), and ten minas (Luke 19:11-27). Following this cue, the first ten brothers form a clan.

The separation of twelve into two groups of ten and two also happened later in a historical moment when Moses sent twelve spies to Canaan. Upon their return, the twelve branched into two groups. One group of ten opposed taking over the land, while the second group of two advocated advance. The ten died in the wilderness, but the two entered the promised land. The two were

Two Clans

Joshua from the tribe of Ephraim, who was blessed by Jacob as the firstborn of Joseph, and Caleb from the tribe of Judah.

In summary, the twelve sons of Jacob represent two clans: the first headed by Judah consisting of the first ten sons, and the second headed by Joseph consisting of two.

The Kingdoms

THE TWO CLANS ARE precursors of two future kingdoms, as evidenced in the final benediction of Genesis chapter 49, where Jacob exuberated over the kingdom of Judah and Joseph. On Judah, Jacob blessed,

> Judah, your brothers will praise you;
> > your hand will be on the neck of your enemies;
> > your father's sons will bow down to you.
> You are a lion's cub, Judah;
> > you return from the prey, my son.
> Like a lion he crouches and lies down,
> > like a lioness—who dares to rouse him
> The scepter will not depart from Judah,
> > nor the ruler's staff from between his feet,
> until he to whom it belongs shall come
> > and the obedience of the nations shall be his.
> He will tether his donkey to a vine,
> > his colt to the choicest branch;
> he will wash his garments in wine,
> > his robes in the blood of grapes.
> His eyes will be darker than wine,
> > his teeth whiter than milk.

The bowing of the brothers established Judah as the head of the family. Judah symbolizes a kingdom because "the scepter will not depart from Judah and the obedience of the nations shall be his." It is noteworthy that, in Joseph's dream, not only his brothers

The Kingdoms

would bow to him but also his parents, the sun and moon, would also bow down. However, in this blessing, only the brothers bow down to Judah. This difference is a telltale sign that the kingdom of Joseph is greater than that of Judah.

On Joseph, Jacob exulted,

> Joseph is a fruitful vine,
>   a fruitful vine near a spring,
>   whose branches climb over a wall.
> With bitterness archers attacked him;
>   they shot at him with hostility.
> But his bow remained steady,
>   his strong arms stayed limber,
> because of the hand of the Mighty One of Jacob,
>   because of the Shepherd, the Rock of Israel,
> because of your father's God, who helps you,
>   because of the Almighty, who blesses you
> with blessings of the skies above,
>   blessings of the deep springs below,
>   blessings of the breast and womb.

Joseph's kingdom is the kingdom backed by God the Almighty, with abundant blessings as high as the sky and as deep as springs. By contrast, God is not mentioned in Judah's kingdom. Thus, Joseph's kingdom is not only greater than Judah's but also exists in a different stratosphere: one on heaven, the other, on earth.

What does Judah's clan symbolize? The spiritual pericopes of the incidents in Jacob's mission years provide hints. The spiritual pericope of the Shechem incident was about God's election, the threat of intermarriage, the covenant of circumcision, and the failure of the elected to be exemplary. Only Judah's clan was involved in this incident because Joseph was only six years old when they crossed Jabbok, and Benjamin was not born yet. In the event of Judah and Tamar, the spiritual pericope was God's words and judgment that gave rise to the concept of righteousness by the law. Thus, the spiritual traits demonstrated by the Shechem and Judah and Tamar stories are exclusively the traits of Judah's clan. Since the aggregate of these spiritual traits—election, the covenant of circumcision, law, and judgment—characterizes the preexilic nation of Israel, Judah's clan in Jacob's life story symbolizes the nation of Israel.

The history of the nation of Israel running through Judah's clan, on one hand, supports the above claim that Judah's clan symbolizes the nation of Israel, and, on the other hand, is perplexing because Jacob considered Joseph as his firstborn son. Of the twelve sons, Joseph received a double portion of the inheritance from Jacob, who said to Joseph,

> I am about to die, but God will be with you and take you back to the land of your fathers. And to you, I give one more ridge of land than to your brothers, the ridge I took from the Amorites with my sword and my bow. (Gen 48:21–22)

Thus, in Jacob's mind, his firstborn son was neither Reuben, who defiled his father's bed, nor Simeon and Levi, who came next to Reuben, because of their violence in Shechem. It was not even Judah who rose to preside over the family, but Joseph, possibly because Rachel was the wife whom Jacob wanted to marry in the first place. So, why didn't the patriarchy of the nation of Israel and the genealogy of Jesus go through Joseph, if he was crowned as the firstborn? Could it be that Judah's clan represents the worldly kingdom and hence continues the worldly history of Israelites? Then, what do Joseph and his clan symbolize? It is time to study the life of Joseph.

Old and New Testament Parallels

To UNDERSTAND THE SPIRITUAL symbolism that Joseph's life stories represent, we parse the major events of his life and extract signature traits. As we proceed from the first to the last story, we build and grow a list of signature traits typical of the stories. Some of the traits may seem trivial at the moment; for instance, Joseph lost his robe, or the cupbearer forgot about Joseph. These details are crucial to tie up the overall argument, and their importance will become apparent when Joseph's life is compared with Jesus' life at the end of the analysis. In the end, all such signature traits define Joseph's role in Jacob's mission years.

The three main events in Joseph's life are (1) his telling of the dream to the brothers that resulted in his being sold to Egypt, (2) his refusal of Potiphar's wife's advances that led to him being jailed, and (3) his interpretation of the dreams of the cupbearer and the baker and Pharaoh that catapulted him to be the governor of Egypt. Further, some of the signature traits have spiritual interpretations, for example, the spiritual symbolism of bread and wine. These interpretations will help understand other events, such as the cup in Benjamin's bag and some references in Jacob's final benediction in Egypt.

Finally, as Jesus said, "These are the very Scriptures that testify about me" (John 5:39), the list of signature traits is used to deduce that Joseph foreshadows Jesus; that is, the signature traits in Joseph's life should have close matches with those in Jesus'.

Together with Judah's symbolism of the nation of Israelites, Jacob's mission years tell us about Jesus, Jews, and God's plan.

A person and events in the Old Testament heralding another person and events in the New Testament is evident in the Bible. Jesus pioneered it. When the Pharisees asked Jesus for a miracle, Jesus replied, "For as Jonah was three days and three nights in the belly of a huge fish, so the Son of Man will be three days and three nights in the heart of the earth. The men of Nineveh will stand up at the judgment with this generation and condemn it; for they repented at the preaching of Jonah, and now something greater than Jonah is here" (Matt 12:40–41). Here Jesus connects Jonah's event to his death and resurrection. In addition to the resurrection event, Jesus also sees the protagonist as a foreshadowing of himself, namely, Jonah to Jesus, and the parallel is between two persons of different greatness: Jesus is greater than Jonah.

The above method of inferring a person in the Old Testament as heralding Jesus is sometimes associated with the technique called typology, which, as Christopher J. H. Wright defines, is a way of understanding Christ and the various events and experiences surrounding him in the New Testament by analogy or correspondence with the historical realities of the Old Testament seen as patterns or models.

The cornerstone for the framework of Jacob's mission years is the parallel interpretation of Joseph as the herald of Jesus. This link between Joseph and Jesus is well established in Christian literature, and the following chapters strengthen this interpretation with additional new insights into the nuances of Joseph's life.

Sheaves and Stars

JOSEPH HAD BEEN QUIET from his birth until he was seventeen years old. Jacob loved Joseph more than any of his other sons and made an ornate robe for him. When his brothers saw that their father loved him more than any of them, they hated him. The hatred intensified when Joseph told them about his two dreams.

> He said to them, "Listen to this dream I had: We were binding sheaves of grain out in the field when suddenly my sheaf rose and stood upright, while your sheaves gathered around mine and bowed down to it."
> His brothers said to him, "Do you intend to reign over us? Will you actually rule us?" And they hated him all the more because of his dream and what he had said.
> Then he had another dream, and he told it to his brothers. "Listen," he said, "I had another dream, and this time the sun and moon and eleven stars were bowing down to me."
> When he told his father as well as his brothers, his father rebuked him and said, "What is this dream you had? Will your mother and I and your brothers actually come and bow down to the ground before you?" His brothers were jealous of him, but his father kept the matter in mind. (Gen 37:6–10)

The two dreams seem to pronounce the message of dominance in the family, but there are nuances in the messages. In the first dream, Joseph and his brothers are all sheaves, whereas, in the second dream, the bowers are celestial objects, and the dream does not identify Joseph as a celestial object, implying the position of Joseph is beyond the celestial domain. Furthermore, the bowers in the second dream include his parents, which elevates Joseph's status beyond the head of the family. Finally, the first dream was fulfilled in Egypt when the brothers bowed before Joseph; but the second was not meant to be fulfilled in this world because Rachel had already died. Besides, Jacob did not bow to Joseph in Egypt. The second dream could mean the person whom Joseph heralded would be worthy of the worship of all in the universe. Because Jacob is one of three patriarchs and Jacob would bow to him, it implies that the status of the person whom Joseph heralded would be beyond humanity.

After Joseph told his brothers about his dream, they hated him all the more. When Joseph wandered to look for them near Dothan, the brothers saw him in the distance and plotted to kill him. "Here comes that dreamer!" they said to each other. "Come now, let us kill him and throw him into one of these cisterns and say that a ferocious animal devoured him. Then we will see what comes of his dreams" (Gen 37:18–20). In effect, the brothers' intent to murder Joseph was motivated by Joseph's claim of prominence.

However, Judah suggested selling him for twenty shekels of silver to Midianites, who then carried him to Egypt.

> So when the Midianite merchants came by, his brothers pulled Joseph up out of the cistern and sold him for twenty shekels of silver to the Ishmaelites, who took him to Egypt.
>
> Then they got Joseph's robe, slaughtered a goat and dipped the robe in the blood. They took the ornate robe back to their father and said, "We found this. Examine it to see whether it is your son's robe."
>
> He recognized it and said, "It is my son's robe! Some ferocious animal has devoured him. Joseph has surely been torn to pieces."
>
> Then Jacob tore his clothes, put on sackcloth and mourned for his son many days. All his sons and daughters came to comfort him, but he refused to be

Sheaves and Stars

comforted. "No," he said, "I will continue to mourn until I join my son in the grave." So his father wept for him. (Gen 37:28, 31–35)

The brothers attempted to kill him but ended up selling him for twenty shekels of silver. To Jacob, Joseph had died because of the blood-stained ornate robe.

Several signature traits are summarized as follows. First, Joseph asserted himself as the head of the family and whom Joseph heralded might be beyond the celestial domain. Second, his brothers' determination to kill him ultimately arose from his self-acclaimed prominence. Third, the brothers sold him for twenty shekels of silver. Finally, Jacob thought Joseph was dead. His brothers also believed his death, as they confessed in their first meeting with Joseph in Egypt.

	Signature Traits of Joseph from Sheaves and Stars
1	Kingship symbolized by the bowing of his brothers and worshiped by all in the universe.
2	Targeted for death as a result of his claim of prominence.
3	Joseph was sold for twenty shekels of silver.
4	All thought Joseph was dead.

Table 1. Traits from sheaves and stars

At Potiphar's House

IN EGYPT, JOSEPH WAS bought by one of Pharaoh's officials, the captain of the guard, Potiphar. God was with him, and Joseph rose from a slave to be the head manager in charge of all affairs in Potiphar's household.

> *The Lord* was with Joseph so that he prospered, and he lived in the house of his Egyptian master. When his master saw that *the Lord* was with him and that *the Lord* gave him success in everything he did, Joseph found favor in his eyes and became his attendant. Potiphar put him in charge of his household, and he entrusted to his care everything he owned. From the time he put him in charge of his household and of all that he owned, *the Lord* blessed the household of the Egyptian because of Joseph. The blessing of *the Lord* was on everything Potiphar had, both in the house and in the field. (Gen 39:2–5)

In the above paragraph, the phrase *the Lord* occurs five times. The presence of God made Joseph succeed in everything he did, and the success spread from Joseph to his surroundings. Because of Joseph, God blessed the household of Potiphar and everything Potiphar had.

Then Potiphar's wife noticed Joseph and seduced him repeatedly, but to no avail. Joseph said to her, "No one is greater in this house than I am. My master has withheld nothing from me except you, because you are his wife. How then could I do such a wicked

At Potiphar's House

thing and sin against God?" (Gen 39:9). Joseph resisted her advance, not because of his fear of being caught, since no one was greater than he was in the house, but because he acknowledged God's ethics.

> One day he went into the house to attend to his duties, and none of the household servants was inside. She caught him by his cloak and said, "Come to bed with me!" But he left his cloak in her hand and ran out of the house.
> When she saw that he had left his cloak in her hand and had run out of the house, she called her household servants and said to them, "this Hebrew has been brought to us to make sport of us! He came in here to sleep with me, but I screamed. When he heard me scream for help, he left his cloak beside me and ran out of the house." (Gen 39:11–12)

She kept his cloak beside her until his master returned home and told him the same. When his master heard the story, he burned with anger and put Joseph in prison, the place where the king's prisoners were confined.

Potiphar's wife accused Joseph *wrongly* and *publicly* as she called out the household servants. As a result, Joseph was jailed. In the struggle with Potiphar's wife, Joseph lost his cloak. In prison, God was with Joseph so that he received favor from the warden, who then made Joseph in charge of all affairs there.

> But while Joseph was there in the prison, *the Lord* was with him; he showed him kindness and granted him favor in the eyes of the prison warden. So the warden put Joseph in charge of all those held in the prison, and he was made responsible for all that was done there. The warden paid no attention to anything under Joseph's care, because *the Lord* was with Joseph and gave him success in whatever he did. (Gen 39:20–23)

Again, what stands out during his prison time is that *the Lord* was with Joseph. Overall, the signature traits in Joseph's tenure in Potiphar's house are: God was with him; Joseph was falsely accused and sent to prison. It is noteworthy that the phrase *the Lord* appears exactly seven times in this chapter, and in all seven times God blessed everything Joseph did. Since the number seven has a special meaning of completeness in the Bible, the seven occurrences of *the Lord* emphasize God's presence with Joseph. Joseph is the first person in the Old Testament whom *the Lord* is associated with seven times.

Finally, Joseph seems to lose his clothes whenever he suffers. When his brothers sold him to Egypt, Joseph lost his ornate robe and again lost his cloak when Potiphar sent him to prison.

Extending on the previous list of signature traits, the new items from this chapter are as follows.

Sheaves and Stars	
1	Kingship symbolized by the bowing of his brothers and worshiped by all in the universe.
2	Targeted for death as a result of his claim of prominence.
3	Joseph was sold for twenty shekels of silver.
4	All thought Joseph was dead.
At Potiphar's House	
5	God was with Joseph; the Lord's name was mentioned seven times.
6	Joseph overcame temptation because he acknowledged God's ethics.
7	Joseph was wrongly accused in public.
8	Joseph lost his clothes before suffering.

Table 2. Traits from Potiphar's house

Cupbearer and Baker

JOSEPH'S FIRST MIRACULOUS DEED was to interpret the dreams of the chief cupbearer and chief baker. Was it a random selection that the cupbearer survived, but the baker did not? Was there a more profound message from the dreams than just a door opener for Joseph to leave the prison? Let's study the passage.

> He asked Pharaoh's officials who were in custody with him in his master's house, "Why do you look so sad today?"
> "We both had dreams," they answered, "but there is no one to interpret them."
> Then Joseph said to them, "Do not interpretations belong to God? Tell me your dreams." (Gen 40:6–8)

This statement from Joseph highlights two crucial points: interpretation of dream comes from God, and Joseph had the confidence that he could receive messages from God. So, Joseph became the first person to perceive messages from God and was self-conscious of his own ability to pronounce them. That is, Joseph was a messenger from God.

> So the chief cupbearer told Joseph his dream. He said to him, "In my dream I saw a vine in front of me, and on the vine were three branches. As soon as it budded, it blossomed, and its clusters ripened into grapes. Pharaoh's cup was in my hand, and I took the grapes, squeezed them into Pharaoh's cup and put the cup in his hand."

> "This is what it means," Joseph said to him. "The three branches are three days. Within three days Pharaoh will lift up your head and restore you to your position, and you will put Pharaoh's cup in his hand, just as you used to do when you were his cupbearer. But when all goes well with you, remember me and show me kindness; mention me to Pharaoh and get me out of this prison. I was forcibly carried off from the land of the Hebrews, and even here I have done nothing to deserve being put in a dungeon."
>
> When the chief baker saw that Joseph had given a favorable interpretation, he said to Joseph, "I too had a dream: On my head were three baskets of bread. In the top basket were all kinds of baked goods for Pharaoh, but the birds were eating them out of the basket on my head."
>
> "This is what it means," Joseph said. "The three baskets are three days. Within three days Pharaoh will lift off your head and impale your body on a pole. And the birds will eat away your flesh."
>
> Now the third day was Pharaoh's birthday, and he gave a feast for all his officials. He lifted up the heads of the chief cupbearer and the chief baker in the presence of his officials: He restored the chief cupbearer to his position, so that he once again put the cup into Pharaoh's hand—but he impaled the chief baker, just as Joseph had said to them in his interpretation. (Gen 40:9–22)

Was the accuracy of Joseph's interpretation the only message in this incident? Was there a deeper meaning associated with the contents of the dreams? In other words, would it matter if the baker, not the cupbearer, or both, survive, as long as Joseph correctly predicted them?

For these questions, the symbolic meanings of bread and wine in the Bible are the keys. Bread may be associated with the human body, as it provides nourishment. However, life is more than just a living body; it has a spirit that uplifts and celebrates life. Thus, in a celebration, both bread and wine are often offered. When Abraham returned from defeating Kedorlaomer and the kings allied with him, Melchizedek, king of Salem, brought out bread and wine for

Abraham (Gen 14:17–18). In the Bible, the spirit feeds not on bread but the words of God, as "man does not live on the bread alone but on every word that comes from the mouth of the Lord" (Deut 8:3).

The New Testament also sheds light on wine's symbolic representation of spirit. Jesus alluded to the Holy Spirit when he taught the parable of the new wine in the old wineskin. In the last supper, Jesus referred to the bread as his body and the wine as his blood of the covenant. "Then he took a cup, and when he had given thanks, he gave it to them, saying, 'Drink from it, all of you. This is my blood of the covenant, which is poured out for many for the forgiveness of sins'" (Matt 26:27–28). The wine here signifies a new covenant, a spiritual entity.

Therefore, bread is symbolic of the body, while wine is symbolic of the spirit. With this understanding, the cupbearer lives because the spirit lives, but the baker, who symbolizes the body, dies. The message in the two dreams, although embedded in the Old Testament, is a New Testament message. As the apostle Paul proclaims in Rom 8:10, "[The] body is subject to death because of sin, the Spirit gives life."

In summary, the signature traits in this episode are below. First, of the two prisoners with Joseph, one lived and the other died. Second, Joseph progressed from seeing God bless him in his work to participating in announcing God's messages through dream interpretation. Joseph pronounced a spiritual principle through symbolism about the death of the flesh and the living of the spirit.

Sheaves and Stars

1	Kingship symbolized by the bowing of his brothers and worshiped by all in the universe.
2	Targeted for death as a result of his claim of prominence.
3	Joseph was sold for twenty shekels of silver.
4	All thought Joseph was dead.

	At Potiphar's House
5	God was with Joseph; the Lord's name was mentioned seven times.
6	Joseph overcame temptation because he acknowledged God's ethics.
7	Joseph was wrongly accused in public.
8	Joseph lost his clothes before suffering.
	Cupbearer and Baker
9	Of the two prisoners with Joseph, one lived, and the other died.
10	Joseph sent the message about living of the spirit and death of the flesh.

Table 3. Traits from the cupbearer and baker

Abandoned

WHEN INTERPRETING THE DREAMS, Joseph probably thought the two officials were God's agents to get him out of prison because he said he was innocent and wanted the cupbearer to mention the dream interpretation to Pharaoh and get him out of prison. However, the chief cupbearer did not remember Joseph; he forgot him. It appears that the cupbearer failed Joseph because of his short-term memory loss; so, God had to come up with a backup plan that made Pharaoh dream two dreams to rescue Joseph.

A bit deeper inspection reveals that it was indeed God's plan that the cupbearer should forget about Joseph the first time. Had the cupbearer remembered Joseph immediately after he was restored by Pharaoh, as Joseph planned, Joseph probably would not be Egypt's governor. Because once the cupbearer mentioned Joseph to Pharaoh, Joseph could be released if the cupbearer were God's agent to free Joseph. So when Pharaoh dreamed of the two dreams, it would be difficult to locate Joseph to interpret. Since God's ultimate goal was not to simply get Joseph out of prison but to elevate him to be the governor of the land, the cupbearer's forgetfulness was in God's plan to keep Joseph in prison so that when the time came, Joseph was readily available.

God could have made Joseph interpret for Pharaoh right after he did for the cupbearer, but God chose to make Joseph wait for two full years. These two years of wait are crucial details that will become clear when Joseph's life is compared with Jesus' life.

Struggle with God and Overcome

Thus, the cupbearer's temporary memory loss and the two-year wait were deliberately planned. During these two years, there was no account of Joseph, who might very well feel abandoned by God following the miracle of interpreting dreams. In many biblical passages, the number two denotes the work of God, and these two years seem to fit the pattern. It can be inferred that the cupbearer's remembrance of Joseph after two full years was also the work of God, just as his forgetfulness upon his release.

"When *two full* years had passed, Pharaoh had a dream . . ." (Gen 41:1). In the *third* year, God raised Joseph from oblivion to greatness.

In summary, the non-accidental memory loss from the cupbearer and the two full years of the wait was in God's plan.

Sheaves and Stars

1	Kingship symbolized by the bowing of his brothers and worshiped by all in the universe.
2	Targeted for death as a result of his claim of prominence.
3	Joseph was sold for twenty shekels of silver.
4	All thought Joseph was dead.

At Potiphar's House

5	God was with Joseph; the Lord's name was mentioned seven times.
6	Joseph overcame temptation because he acknowledged God's ethics.
7	Joseph was wrongly accused in public.
8	Joseph lost his clothes before suffering.

Cupbearer and Baker

9	Of the two prisoners with Joseph, one lived, and the other died.
10	Joseph sent the message about living of the spirit and death of the flesh.

Abandoned

11	God planned that the cupbearer abandoned Joseph for two years.
12	In the third year, God raised up Joseph.

Table 4. Traits from abandoned

Pharaoh's Dreams

TWO FULL YEARS HAD passed since Joseph interpreted the dreams for the cupbearer and baker. Pharaoh had two dreams that no Egyptian was able to interpret.

> He was standing by the *Nile*, when out of the river there came up seven cows, sleek and fat, and they grazed among the reeds. After them, seven other cows, ugly and gaunt, came up out of the Nile and stood beside those on the riverbank. And the cows that were ugly and gaunt ate up the seven sleek, fat cows. Then Pharaoh woke up.
> He fell asleep again and had a second dream: Seven heads of grain, healthy and good, were growing on a single stalk. After them, seven other heads of grain sprouted—thin and scorched by the east wind. The thin heads of grain swallowed up the seven healthy, full heads. Then Pharaoh woke up; it had been a dream.
> In the morning his mind was troubled, so he sent for all the magicians and wise men of Egypt. Pharaoh told them his dreams, but no one could interpret them for him. (Gen 41:1-8)

So far, there are three pairs of dreams that Joseph has dealt with: (1) the dreams about bowing to himself, (2) the dreams from the cupbearer and the baker, and (3) the dreams from Pharaoh himself. Pharaoh's dreams differ from the previous ones because they are locale specific, namely, the Nile, whereas the previous ones have no such indication. This information may imply that Pharaoh's dreams are only meant for Egypt at the time, not to have a more general meaning beyond the scope.

Now the cupbearer remembered Joseph and told Pharaoh how Joseph correctly interpreted the dreams. Joseph was sent before Pharaoh. "Pharaoh said to Joseph, 'I had a dream, and no one can interpret it. But I have heard it said of you that when you hear a dream you can interpret it.' 'I cannot do it,' Joseph replied to Pharaoh, 'but God will give Pharaoh the answer he desires.'" With that, Joseph pronounced himself as a messenger of God and that his rise to greatness came solely from God.

Then, Pharaoh repeated the two dreams to Joseph, emphasizing the location, "I had never seen such ugly cows in all the land of *Egypt*."

> Then Joseph said to Pharaoh, "The dreams of Pharaoh are *one and the same*. God has revealed to Pharaoh what he is about to do. The seven good cows are seven years, and the seven good heads of grain are seven years; it is *one and the same* dream. The seven lean, ugly cows that came up afterward are seven years, and so are the seven worthless heads of grain scorched by the east wind: They are seven years of famine.
> ... "Seven years of great abundance are coming throughout the land of Egypt, but seven years of famine will follow them ... The reason the dream was given to Pharaoh in two forms is that the matter has been firmly decided by God, and God will do it soon." (Gen 41:25–32)

Joseph had two dreams of his brothers and family bowing to him. These two dreams are similar but different. The first one of the sheaves was fulfilled in Egypt, but the second one of greater significance was not meant to be fulfilled in this world as one parent, Rachel, had already died. Further, the cupbearer and the baker had similar dreams but opposite meanings and outcomes.

Because the cupbearer told Pharaoh about how his and the baker's dreams turned out differently, Joseph emphasized twice that Pharaoh's two dreams were the same and the reason for the two forms was to show the matter had been firmly decided by God, and God would do it soon. "One as the same," together with the locale specificity, i.e., Nile and Egypt, implies that the dreams were meant for Egypt only at the specific time, not having a more general and different implication as in Joseph's two dreams.

Besides interpreting the dreams, Joseph advised Pharaoh on how Egypt could be saved from famine.

> And now let Pharaoh look for a discerning and wise man and put him in charge of the land of Egypt ... They should collect all the food of these good years ... should be held in reserve for the country, to be used during the seven years of famine that will come upon Egypt, so that the country may not be ruined by the famine. (Gen 41:33–36)

Pharaoh was satisfied with Joseph's interpretation and advice and made him be in charge of the land of Egypt as "his second-in-command," because, "Can we find anyone like this man, one in whom is the spirit of God?" (Gen 41:43, 38). Here, Pharaoh acknowledged that Joseph was God's plan messenger and executor.

Joseph was thirty years old when he entered the service of Pharaoh king of Egypt (Gen 41:46).

In summary, the signature traits in this episode are fourfold. First, it was made explicit to all that God's spirit was with Joseph, and God's power manifested in elevating Joseph from dungeon to dignity. As such, God took on the central stage with Joseph being his interpreter or messenger, a progression from previous events in which God blessed Joseph "on the sideline." Second, Joseph laid out a plan to save Egypt. Third, Joseph rose to the second-in-command to Pharaoh. Finally, Joseph was thirty years old when he entered the service of Pharaoh. Append the following new traits to the list above.

Pharaoh's Dreams

Sheaves and Stars

1	Kingship symbolized by the bowing of his brothers and worshiped by all in the universe.
2	Targeted for death as a result of his claim of prominence.
3	Joseph was sold for twenty shekels of silver.
4	All thought Joseph was dead.

At Potiphar's House

5	God was with Joseph; the Lord's name was mentioned seven times.
6	Joseph overcame temptation because he acknowledged God's ethics.
7	Joseph was wrongly accused in public.
8	Joseph lost his clothes before suffering.

Cupbearer and Baker

9	Of the two prisoners with Joseph, one lived, and the other died.
10	Joseph sent the message about living of the spirit and death of the flesh.

Abandoned

11	God planned that the cupbearer abandoned Joseph for two years.
12	In the third year, God raised up Joseph.

	Pharaoh's Dreams
13	The explicit manifestation of God's power in raising Joseph to greatness.
14	Joseph laid out the plan to save Egypt.
15	Joseph was the second-in-command to Pharaoh.
16	Joseph was thirty years ago when he entered the service of Pharaoh.

Table 5. Traits from Pharaoh's dreams

Joseph and Jesus

THUS FAR, JOSEPH'S LIFE stories have been analyzed for signature traits before the reunions with his brothers. Based on this list, we can see all of Joseph's signature traits in Jesus' life, as examined below. Thus, Joseph's life heralds the coming of Jesus. To proceed with this analysis, we arrange the list by order of the events recorded in the New Testament and compare it with a similar trait in Jesus' life for each Joseph's trait. If all signature traits of Joseph match with those in Jesus' life, we infer that Joseph's life heralds the coming of Jesus.

Signature Traits of Joseph

1	God was with Joseph; the Lord's name was mentioned seven times.
2	Joseph was thirty years ago when he entered the service of Pharaoh.
3	Joseph overcame temptation because he acknowledged God's ethics.
4	Joseph sent the message about living of the spirit and death of the flesh.
5	Joseph laid out the plan to save Egypt.
6	Targeted for death as a result of his claim of prominence.

Struggle with God and Overcome

Signature Traits of Joseph

7	Joseph was wrongly accused in public.
8	Joseph was sold for twenty shekels of silver.
9	Of the two prisoners with Joseph, one lived and the other died.
10	Joseph lost his clothes before suffering.
11	All thought Joseph was dead.
12	God planned that the cupbearer abandoned Joseph for two years.
13	In the third year, God raised up Joseph.
14	The explicit manifestation of God's power in raising Joseph to greatness.
15	Joseph was the second-in-command to Pharaoh.
16	Kingship symbolized by the bowing of his brothers and worshiped by all in the universe.

Table 6. Summary of Joseph's signature traits arranged in NT order

One by one, we will study Joseph's signature traits in Jesus.

1. **God was with Joseph; the Lord's name was mentioned seven times.**

   After Jesus was baptized, he prayed, and heaven opened. The Holy Spirit descended on him in bodily form like a dove. Since then, the Spirit never left Jesus. As Nicodemus said to Jesus, "Rabbi, we know that you are a teacher who has come from God. For no one could perform the signs you are doing if God were not with him" (John 3:2).

2. **Joseph was thirty years old when he entered the service of Pharaoh.**
   Jesus began his ministry when he was about thirty years old (Luke 3:21–23).

3. **Joseph overcame temptation because he acknowledged God's ethics.**
   After baptism, Jesus was led by the Spirit into the wilderness, where for forty days he was tempted by the devil. Jesus overcame the temptations by referring to God's ethics, e.g., "Worship the Lord your God and serve him only." And "Do not put the Lord your God to the test" (Luke 4:1–13).

4. **Joseph sent the message about living of the spirit and death of the flesh.**
   In prison, Joseph pronounced that the cupbearer would live and the baker would die. With reference to bread as the body and wine as the spirit, Joseph announced the message that the body died, but the spirit gave life. In response to the devil's temptation to turn stones into bread, Jesus answered, "Man shall not live on bread alone" (Matt 4:4). In other words, living on bread alone will die, but the spirit gives life.

   Regarding wine, Jesus used wine as a metaphor for the new covenant of forgiveness. In the last supper, Jesus took a cup, and when he had given thanks, he gave it to them, saying, "Drink from it, all of you. This is my blood of the covenant, which is poured out for many for the forgiveness of sins" (Matt 26:27–28). Therefore, the message symbolic of bread and wine in Joseph's story was a shadow of Jesus' messages, which can be summed up in Rom 8:13: "For if you live according to the flesh, you will die; but if by the Spirit you put to death the misdeeds of the body, you will live."

5. **Joseph laid out the plan to save Egypt.**
   Jesus wanted to save the Israelites from ruin by receiving him as the Messiah. He said, "how often I have longed to gather your children together, as a hen gathers her chicks under her wings, and you were not willing. Look, your house is left to

you desolate. For I tell you, you will not see me again until you say, 'Blessed is he who comes in the name of the Lord'" (Matt 23:37–39).

6. **Targeted for death as a result of his claim of prominence.**
Joseph's brothers' intent to murder Joseph was motivated by Joseph's claim of prominence. Similarly, one of the reasons that Jews plotted to kill Jesus was Jesus' claim as Messiah. Jesus was brought before the Sanhedrin, and the chief priests and the whole Sanhedrin were looking for false evidence against Jesus so that they could put him to death. However, they did not find any, though many false witnesses came forward. Then the high priest said to him, "I charge you under oath by the living God: Tell us if you are the Messiah, the Son of God." "You have said so," Jesus replied. "But I say to all of you: From now on you will see the Son of Man sitting at the right hand of the Mighty One and coming on the clouds of heaven." Then the high priest tore his clothes and said, "He has spoken blasphemy! Why do we need any more witnesses? Look, now you have heard the blasphemy. What do you think?" "He is worthy of death," they answered (Matt 26:59–65).

7. **Joseph was wrongly accused in public.**
When Jesus was tried before the Roman court, Pilate asked, "Do you want me to release to you the king of the Jews?" knowing it was out of self-interest that the chief priests had handed Jesus over to him. But the chief priests stirred up the crowd to have Pilate release Barabbas instead. "What shall I do, then, with the one you call the king of the Jews?" Pilate asked them. "Crucify him!" they shouted (Mark 15:9–13). Jesus was found innocent of all charges put forward by the Jews, as Pilate announced to the chief priests and the crowd, "I find no basis for a charge against this man" (Luke 23:4). Nevertheless, Pilate gave him to the crowd who shouted out, "His blood is on us and our children!" (Matt 27:25). Similarly, Joseph was falsely accused by Potiphar's wife in public and sent to prison.

8. **Joseph was sold for twenty shekels of silver.**
Jesus was sold for thirty pieces of silver (Matt 26:15). The price for a slave had increased over the years.

9. **Of the two prisoners with Joseph, one lived, and the other died.**
Joseph met two prisoners and announced that the cupbearer would live while the other, the baker, would die. Similarly, on the cross, Jesus was with two criminals and pronounced that one would be in paradise and the other lost (Luke 23:43).

10. **Joseph lost his clothes before suffering.**
Joseph lost his robe and cloak in his sufferings when sold to Egypt and again when he fled from Potiphar's wife. At the cross, soldiers divided Jesus' clothes among themselves (John 19:23).

11. **All thought Joseph was dead.**
Joseph's brother sold him but told Jacob that Joseph was dead, and then they later believed that Joseph was indeed dead until he revealed himself. This scenario also happened in Jesus' case. Even the women who saw Jesus' resurrection told the chief priests about it, the chief told the grave guarding soldiers about Jesus' death and the story since has been widely circulated among the Jews to this day (Matt 28:11–15).

12. **God planned that the cupbearer abandoned Joseph for two years.**
As a part of God's plan, the cupbearer forgot about Joseph to keep him in prison so that he could be summoned immediately when Pharaoh had the dream. Joseph had to wait for two years to leave prison. Joseph witnessed firsthand God's involvement when he correctly interpreted the dreams of the cupbearer and baker and then experienced a seeming failure of God's rescue plan. This two-year period would seem to Joseph the darkest time that God had abandoned him, as indicated by the lack of any mention of Joseph. In the darkest hour on the cross, Jesus cried out in a loud voice, "Eloi, Eloi,

lema sabachthani?" (which means "My God, my God, why have you forsaken me?") (Mark 15:34).

13. **In the third year, God raised up Joseph.**
    On the third day, Jesus rose from death. When women went to Jesus' tomb, two angels told them that "the Son of Man must be delivered over to the hands of sinners, be crucified and on the third day be raised again" (Luke 24:7).

14. **The explicit manifestation of God's power in raising Joseph to greatness.**
    Joseph's rise to greatness came from God, as he acknowledged before Pharaoh's assembly. "I cannot do it, but God will give Pharaoh the answer he desires" (Gen 41:16). Jesus' rise from death is the work of God, as an angel told Mary Magdalene and Mary the mother of James and Salome, "He has risen!" (Mark 16:1–7). The the apostle Peter told the high priest before the Sanhedrin, "The God of our ancestors raised Jesus from the dead—whom you killed by hanging him on a cross" (Acts 5:30).

15. **Joseph was the second-in-command to Pharaoh.**
    Joseph's becoming the second-in-command to Pharaoh foretold Jesus' rising to be "seated at the right hand of the mighty God" (Luke 22:69).

16. **Kingship symbolized by the bowing of his brothers and worshiped by all in the universe.**
    After the resurrection, Jesus appeared to the eleven disciples and said, "All authority in heaven and on earth has been given to me" (Matt 28:18). The apostle Paul wrote, "At the name of Jesus every knee should bow, in heaven and on earth and under the earth, and every tongue acknowledge that Jesus Christ is Lord, to the glory of God the Father" (Phil 2:10–11). The celestial version of Joseph's bowing dream was to be fulfilled by Jesus.

Joseph and Jesus

The following table summarizes the signature trait comparison.

Signature Trait Comparison between Joseph and Jesus

	Joseph	Jesus
1	God was with him.	God's Spirit was with Jesus. (Matt 3:16, John, 3:2)
2	Was thirty years ago when he entered the service of Pharaoh.	Was thirty when he started his ministry. (Luke 3:23)
3	Joseph overcame temptation because he acknowledged God's ethics.	Overcame devil's temptations in the wilderness using God's words. (Matt 4)
4	Joseph sent the message about living of the spirit and death of the flesh.	Taught about living was more than bread and the cup representing the covenant of forgiveness. (Matt 4:4, 26:27–28)
5	Joseph laid out the plan to save Egypt.	Jesus wanted to save the Israelites by receiving him as the Messiah. (Matt 23:37–39)
6	Targeted for death as a result of his claim of prominence.	Acknowledged as Messiah, Son of God and Jews plotted to kill him. (Matt 26:59–66)
7	Joseph was wrongly accused in public.	Pilate declared Jesus innocent but still gave him to Jews. (Luke 23:4)
8	Sold for twenty shekels of silver.	Judas sold Jesus for 30 pieces of silver. (Matt 26:15)
9	Of the two prisoners with Joseph, one (cupbearer) lived, and the other (baker) died.	Of the two criminals at the cross with Jesus, Jesus said one would be in paradise. (Luke 23:43)

Signature Trait Comparison between Joseph and Jesus

	Joseph	Jesus
10	Joseph lost his clothes before suffering.	Soldiers divided Jesus' clothes. (John 19:23)
11	All thought Joseph was dead.	Chief priests spread a rumor about Jesus' death which lasts till today. (Matt 28:11–15)
12	God planned that the cupbearer abandoned Joseph.	Jesus cried loudly, "My God, my God, why have you forsaken me?" (Mark 15:34)
13	In the third year, God raised up Joseph.	On the third day, Jesus rose from death. (Luke 24:7)
14	The explicit manifestation of God's power in raising Joseph to greatness.	Jesus rose from death by the power of God. (Acts 5:30)
15	Joseph was the second-in-command to Pharaoh.	Jesus seated at the right hand of the might God. (Luke 22:69)
16	Kingship symbolized by the bowing of his family and all in the universe.	All authority in heaven and on earth has been given to Jesus. (Matt 28:18)

Table 7. Summary of Joseph and Jesus signature traits comparison

In summary, Joseph's life story foretold the coming of Jesus. Since Judah and the other nine brothers symbolize the nation of Israel, how Joseph interacted with his brothers later in Egypt should also be indicative of how Jesus interacted with Jews in the New Testament. Therefore, their reunions serve as the benchmark to test this parallel hypothesis against the accounts in the New Testament. In fact, the comparison between the two reunions in Egypt with Jesus' two comings in the New Testament will reinforce the hypothesis.

Staging

BEFORE GETTING INTO THE reunion of Joseph with his brothers, we review what we have studied so far. The overall result is summarized in figure 8. The bottom half of the figure is shaded to represent the nation of Israel, and the upper half, a new nation of God. Both nations originate from the same twelve tribes. The two clans, heralding the two nations, branch out after the Shechem incident. Below each event is a summary of the key messages derived from it. For example, in the incident of Dinah at Shechem, a central theme is God's election of his people and the covenant of circumcision, and how the elected failed to respond to threats. When the elected lived among the nations, a threat came in the form of intermarriage. The elected in the case responded with deceit and cruelty, a presage of the elected people's failure before God's mandates.

In the forming of the twelve tribes, the two incidents, Reuben sleeping with Bilhah and the death of Rachel, complete the membership of the tribes.

Then the twelve tribes split into two clans divided by daughter Dinah, one consisting of the first ten brothers and the other, the rest. Judah heads the first clan, Joseph, the other. The Judah clan represents the nation of Israel, as marked by election, the covenant of circumcision, and law—the backbone characteristic of the nation of Israel. The Joseph clan represents a new nation of God.

Struggle with God and Overcome

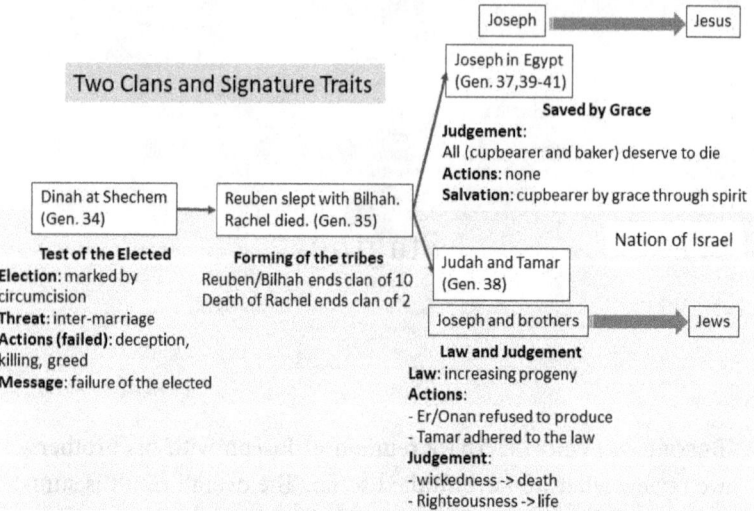

Figure 8. Two clans and signature messages

The heads of the clans departed simultaneously from each other and journeyed on their paths.

In Judah's life path, people lived and died by the law. Er and Onan were deemed wicked and struck down by God because they refused to proliferate in accordance with God's words. By the same token, Tamar was deemed righteous as she fulfilled her duty to extend the family lineage. Judah failed the temptation as he mistook Tamar for a prostitute. The story of Judah and Tamar typifies his clan and the nation of Israel, law and judgment. God displayed judgment for the first time to the patriarchal family and demonstrated the spiritual concept of righteousness before the law and the consequences.

In Joseph's life path, all people deserved to die, but some were saved by providence or grace, not by their deeds. The motif incident is the cupbearer and the baker. Both the cupbearer and the baker were under the wrath of Pharaoh and deserved to die. The cupbearer survived because of providence through the spirit symbolized by wine. Thus, this story signified the salvific principle in the gospel. Further, Joseph lived an unblemished life. He was mistreated and slandered. He overcame the temptation from Potiphar's wife. Yet God was with him and blessed whatever he did. Eventually, God raised him from oblivion to be Egypt's governor. Joseph's unblemished life foreshadows the coming of Jesus, and Joseph's clan, a new nation of God.

The reunion of Joseph and his brothers was the apex in the lives of Jacob, Joseph, and his brothers, because it brought all parties together to face the wrongs and reconcile, because it erased the pains and losses of the past, and because it prophesized the fate of the nation of Israel and the new nation of God.

Famine

As described in Pharaoh's dreams, seven years of great harvest was followed by a famine. During the seven years of abundance, Joseph stored up a huge amount of grain in the fields, like the sand of the sea, so much that he stopped keeping records because it was beyond measure. When the seven years of famine started, it swept throughout all the lands, but only Egypt had food. Then Joseph opened all the storehouses and sold grain to the Egyptians. Soon, people from all over the world came to Egypt for food.

On the one hand, when Jacob left Laban, he was wealthy, owning large flocks, camels, donkeys, and servants (Gen 30:43), just like Abraham and Isaac, who were "very wealthy in livestock and in silver and gold" (Gen 13:2) and had many flocks and herds and servants (Gen 26:14). On the other hand, unlike Abraham and Isaac, whose wealth sustained their lives, Jacob faced a severe famine that was threatening the family's livelihood. It is this disaster that turned around Jacob's suffering.

Jacob learned that there was grain in Egypt and sent ten sons there to buy grain. The trip to Egypt set the stage for the reunion between Joseph and his brothers. As it turned out, the reunion took two trips; so, the first trip will be called the first reunion, the second trip, the second reunion. We posit that the two reunions are emblematic of Jesus' first and second coming. Thus, in the following discussion, we study the signature traits of the reunions and connect them to signature events in Jesus' first and second coming.

First Reunion

JACOB SENT TEN SONS to Egypt to buy grain, keeping Benjamin at home for fear that harm would come to him. The absence of Benjamin in the first reunion and his central role in the second reunion are critical cues in identifying the group that Benjamin heralds and establishing the nexus between the two reunions and Jesus' two comings.

> So when Joseph's brothers arrived, they bowed down to him with their faces to the ground. As soon as Joseph saw his brothers, he recognized them, but he pretended to be a stranger and spoke harshly to them. "Where do you come from?" he asked.
> "From the land of Canaan," they replied, "to buy food."
> Although Joseph recognized his brothers, they did not recognize him. (Gen 42:6–8)

Joseph's first dream of sheaves was fulfilled when the brothers arrived in Egypt and bowed to him. Joseph immediately recognized his brothers, but they did not recognize him. The brother recognized Joseph only as a powerful person but not as their own brother.

> Then he remembered his dreams about them and said to them, "You are spies! You have come to see where our land is unprotected."
> . . .

> But they replied, "Your servants were twelve brothers, the sons of one man, who lives in the land of Canaan. The youngest is now with our father, and one is no more." (Gen 42:9–13)

Why did Joseph call them spies? That accusation forced the brothers to talk about themselves to clear their names. The conversation then led to their family and the other brothers not being present with them; "The youngest is now with our father, and one is no more." Joseph successfully directed the brothers' attention to the other two brothers, Benjamin and Joseph.

Next, Joseph asked them to validate their claim by sending one back home to bring in Benjamin while nine stayed in Egypt. Joseph then put the brothers in custody for three days. Later, Joseph changed his mind.

> On the third day, Joseph said to them, ". . . If you are honest men, let one of your brothers stay here in prison, while the rest of you go and take grain back for your starving households. But you must bring your youngest brother to me, so that your words may be verified and that you may not die." (Gen 42:18–19)

Retaining nine brothers rather than one, on the one hand, would ensure a better chance of getting Benjamin to Egypt, but on the other hand, it would be less convincing to demonstrate their honesty. As a matter of fact, even retaining one brother was not necessary because the famine would force them to return. Thus, as discussed later, Joseph held on to one brother not as a hostage, as it appeared to be, but for a different purpose.

Why did Joseph insist on bringing in Benjamin? The favoritism that Jacob showed toward Joseph stirred up hatred from the other ten brothers. "Israel loved Joseph more than any of his other sons because he had been born to him in his old age; and he made an ornate robe for him. When his brothers saw that their father loved him more than any of them, they hated him and could not speak a kind word to him" (Gen 37:3–4). The hatred turned into the abduction of Joseph. Jacob continued to show favoritism toward Benjamin, keeping him alone at home while sending the other ten

First Reunion

sons out buying food. Getting Benjamin to Egypt, away from Jacob, would give the brothers another opportunity to avenge or redeem themselves, which will be seen more clearly in the second reunion.

> They said to one another, "Surely we are being punished because of our brother. We saw how distressed he was when he pleaded with us for his life, but we would not listen; that's why this distress has come on us."
>
> Reuben replied, "Didn't I tell you not to sin against the boy? But you wouldn't listen! Now we must give an accounting for his blood." (Gen 42:18–23)

The suffering in prison and the harsh demand for verification prompted them to think of punishment for something they did. They immediately recalled their selling of Joseph and regretted it. "Surely we are being punished because of our brother."

Then, Joseph had Simeon taken from them and bound before their eyes (Gen 42:24). Why chose Simeon? Choosing Simeon was to confirm the brothers' conclusion that their problem on hand had to do with their mistreatment of Joseph for the following reasons. If the person to stay were to represent the group, Reuben would be chosen as he was the eldest and the head of the group. Since Reuben was not chosen, the selection criterion was more than just representing the group but relating to Joseph's abduction, which the brothers came to realize. Under this criterion, Reuben was not chosen because he was not involved. On the contrary, Reuben wanted to rescue Joseph. Simeon was picked, probably because he played a leading role in the plot to kill Joseph. At the time, he was the eldest brother as Reuben was not among them, and Simeon's inclination for violence was evident in the Shechem killing. Therefore, Simeon was retained to affirm the brothers' understanding of the situation instead of as a hostage for their return because the famine would drive them back later.

> Joseph gave orders to fill their bags with grain, to put each man's silver back in his sack, and to give them provisions for their journey . . .
>
> At the place where they stopped for the night one of them opened his sack to get feed for his donkey, and he

saw his silver in the mouth of his sack. "My silver has been returned," he said to his brothers. "Here it is in my sack."

Their hearts sank and they turned to each other trembling and said, "What is this that God has done to us?" (Gen 42:25–28)

Getting grain and silver returned was unthinkable, even stressful, for them. Throughout their lives, they had to fight for properties with Laban's family and the men in Shechem. What the brothers got was a grace that saved lives.

When they found out, their hearts sank, and they said, "What is this that God has done to us?" In all accounts of the nine brothers, this was the very first time they mentioned God, not even when they tricked the Shechemites to circumcise, using a mandate from God for the elect.

In summary, there are five signature traits in the first reunion. First, Benjamin was not on the trip. Second, Joseph recognized the ten brothers, but they only recognized him as an authority figure but not his true identity. Third, the ten brothers were made aware of their selling of Joseph and felt they were punished for their deeds. Fourth, a second trip was preannounced with Benjamin reuniting with Joseph. Finally, their silvers were returned. By grace, they received lifesaving food, and the brothers associated it with God.

Signature Traits of the First Reunion

1	Benjamin was absent.
2	Joseph recognized his brothers but they did not recognize him.
3	Joseph reminded the brothers of their sins.
4	The second trip was announced and predicated on Benjamin's coming.
5	All silvers were returned.

Table 8. Characteristics of the first reunion

First Coming

THE FIRST REUNION WITH Joseph heralds the first coming of Jesus because the above five signature traits are evident in Jesus' ministry.

First, as symbolized by Benjamin, the new nation of God was absent in Jesus' first coming. In sending his disciples, Jesus gave them the instructions, "Do not go among the Gentiles or enter any town of the Samaritans. Go rather to the lost sheep of Israel" (Matt 10:5–6). In his encounter with a Canaanite woman, who asked Jesus to heal her demon-possessed daughter, Jesus replied, "I was sent only to the lost sheep of Israel" (Matt 15:24). Therefore, the nation of Israel, symbolized by Judah's clan, was the focus of Jesus' ministry in his first coming.

Second, Joseph's brothers saw Joseph's authority but did not know his true identity. Similarly, Jews marveled at the many miracles that Jesus performed but failed to recognize Jesus' true identity, the Messiah. For instance, when a demon-possessed man who could not talk was brought to Jesus, Jesus drove out the demon, and the man spoke. The crowd was amazed and said, "Nothing like this has ever been seen in Israel." But the Pharisees said, "It is by the prince of demons that he drives out demons" (Matt 9:32–34).

In addition to miracles, Jews saw the authority with which Jesus taught in a synagogue but spurned him. When Jesus taught in the synagogue, many who heard him were amazed. "Where did this man get these things?" they asked. "What's this wisdom that has been given him? What are these remarkable miracles he is performing? Isn't this the carpenter? Isn't this Mary's son and the brother of James, Joseph, Judas, and Simon? Aren't his sisters here with us?" And they took offense at him (Mark 6:2–3).

Further, when Jesus was brought before Sanhedrin, the high priest said to him, "I charge you under oath by the living God: Tell us if you are the Messiah, the Son of God." "You have said so," Jesus replied. "But I say to all of you: From now on you will see the Son of Man sitting at the right hand of the Mighty One and coming on the clouds of heaven." Then the high priest tore his clothes and said, "He has spoken blasphemy!" (Matt 26:63–65).

Third, just like the case in Egypt where Joseph's exchanges with his brothers reminded them of their wrongdoings, Jesus preached repentance to the Jews. "After John was put in prison, Jesus went into Galilee, proclaiming the good news of God. 'The time has come,' he said. 'The kingdom of God has come near. Repent and believe the good news!'" (Mark 1:14–15).

Instead of directly pointing out the brothers' past in the union, Joseph asked about the youngest brother Benjamin and thus invoked the brothers' memory of their killing of the father's favorite son. Selecting Simeon to stay behind confirmed the brothers' speculations about their killing of Joseph. Similarly, Jesus spoke in parables to the Jewish leaders about their evil behavior. The parable of the tenants invokes a clear parallel to Joseph's story: a favorite son was killed by the hired hands, and the Jewish leaders understood the parable.

> Jesus then began to speak to them in parables: "A man planted a vineyard. He put a wall around it, dug a pit for the winepress, and built a watchtower. Then he rented the vineyard to some farmers and moved to another place. At harvest time he sent a servant to the tenants to collect from them some of the fruit of the vineyard. But they seized him, beat him, and sent him away empty-handed. Then he sent another servant to them; they struck this man on the head and treated him shamefully. He sent still another, and that one they killed. He sent many others; some of them they beat, others they killed.

"He had one left to send, a son, whom he loved. He sent him last of all, saying, 'They will respect my son.'

"But the tenants said to one another, 'This is the heir. Come, let's kill him, and the inheritance will be ours.' So they took him and killed him, and threw him out of the vineyard.

"What then will the owner of the vineyard do? He will come and kill those tenants and give the vineyard to others. Haven't you read this passage of Scripture:

"'The stone the builders rejected
has become the cornerstone;
the Lord has done this,
and it is marvelous in our eyes?'"

Then the chief priests, the teachers of the law, and the elders looked for a way to arrest him because they knew he had spoken the parable against them. (Mark 12:1–12)

Fourth, Joseph preannounced a second trip, and the condition was that Benjamin must come along. Jesus predicted his second coming, "For I tell you, you will not see me again until you say, 'Blessed is he who comes in the name of the Lord'" (Matt 23:39). The condition is Jesus' pronouncement that the Jews must acknowledge the one who comes in the name of the Lord. This pronouncement means that, in Jesus' second coming, the Jews will be together with the group that Benjamin symbolizes, and the Jews' reception of the group is tantamount to receiving Jesus. Jesus hinted about this group when he taught, "I have other sheep that are not of this sheep pen. I must bring them also. They too will listen to my voice, and there shall be one flock and one shepherd" (John 10:16). "At that time they will see the Son of Man coming in a cloud with power and great glory" (Luke 21:27).

Finally, as Joseph commanded to return the silvers to nine brothers, the brothers received the lifesaving provision as a grace. Further, the source of grace from God was made explicit in Joseph's story. Upon seeing the silver in their sacks, the brothers immediately associated that with God, although they thought it was an omen of God's punishment.

The message of salvation by grace is pervasive throughout the books of the gospel. Jesus preached grace from God, performing healing miracles on all who came. To sum it up, Jesus said to the disciples, "Go into all the world and preach the gospel to all creation. Whoever believes and is baptized will be saved, but whoever does not believe will be condemned" (Mark 16:15–16).

	Joseph and Brothers' First Reunion	Jesus' First Coming
1	Benjamin was absent.	Ministry to Jews only, no gentiles.
2	Joseph recognized his brothers but they did not recognize him.	Jews did not recognize Jesus.
3	Joseph reminded the brothers of their sins.	Jesus preached repentance of sins.
4	The second trip was announced and predicated on Benjamin's coming.	Jesus proclaimed his second coming and Jews would welcome him and those who call on Jesus.
5	All silvers were returned.	Jesus preached the grace from God.

Table 9. Comparison of Joseph's first reunion and Jesus' first coming

Therefore, the first reunion of Joseph with Judah's clan foreshadows Jesus's first coming to the nation of Israel. This analysis is summarized in figure 9. The horizontal arrows denote parallel between the persons, for example, Joseph heralds Jesus. The five elements in each middle box correspond to their counterparts. To conclude, the five significant features in the first reunion have resounding correspondences in Jesus' ministry to Jews and thus strengthen the parallel hypothesis of Joseph and Judah's clan with Jesus and Jews, respectively.

First Coming

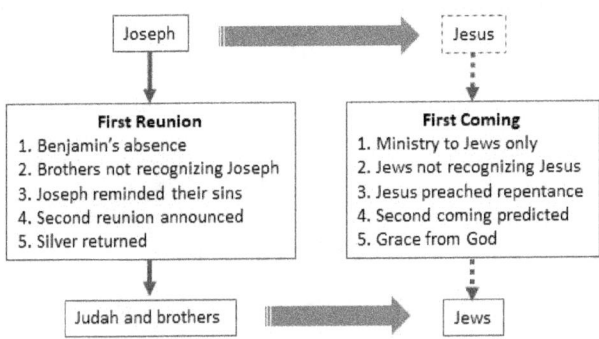

Joseph's First Reunions and Jesus' First Coming

Figure 9. Comparing Joseph's first reunion with Jesus' first coming

Second Reunion

As Jacob's family ran out of food, they decided to return to Egypt to get more grain. However, Judah said to Jacob that "the man warned us solemnly, 'You will not see my face again unless your brother is with you'" (Gen 43:3, 5). After much struggle and with Judah's guarantee of Benjamin's safe return, Jacob finally agreed to let Benjamin go with the nine brothers.

The group brought extra silver to cover the returned ones and explained to Joseph's steward that they had paid but later found the silvers in the sacks. The steward reiterated God as the source of grace, "Don't be afraid. Your God, the God of your father, has given you treasure in your sacks; I received your silver" (Gen 43:23).

The ten brothers and Benjamin met and had a banquet in Joseph's house. At the banquet, Benjamin was given five times the portion as anyone else's.

> Now Joseph gave these instructions to the steward of his house: "Fill the men's sacks with as much food as they can carry, and put each man's silver in the mouth of his sack. Then put my cup, the silver one, in the mouth of the youngest one's sack, along with the silver for his grain." And he did as Joseph said. (Gen 44:1–2)

The silver from the brothers had been returned a second time because, in Joseph's words, "The reason . . . in two forms is that the matter has been firmly decided by God, and God will do it soon"

SECOND REUNION

(Gen 41:32). As discussed previously, returning the silver signified the salvific grace from God, and the grace was emphasized through repetition.

Shortly after the caravan left, Joseph had the steward go after the group to search for the cup. When the steward caught up with them, the steward did as Joseph ordered, despite objections from the brothers.

> Then the steward proceeded to search, beginning with the oldest and ending with the youngest. And the cup was found in Benjamin's sack. At this, they tore their clothes. Then they all loaded their donkeys and returned to the city. (Gen 44:12–13)

Back at Joseph's house, Joseph wanted to retain Benjamin only and sent the others home instead of keeping all brothers as slaves.

> What can we say? How can we prove our innocence? God has uncovered your servants' guilt. We are now my lord's slaves—we ourselves and the one who was found to have the cup. (Gen 44:16)

At this point, Judah emerged as the group leader and spoke for the brothers. He acknowledged that God had uncovered their guilt on Joseph. Further, throughout the years since Joseph's disappearance, the brothers changed, and their repentance resulted in their changed attitude toward Jacob's favorite sons. Now they stood together with Benjamin and were willing to serve as slaves.

> But Joseph said, "Far be it from me to do such a thing! Only the man who was found to have the cup will become my slave. The rest of you, go back to your father in peace." (Gen 44:17)

Jacob's favoritism toward Joseph was the very reason that kindled the brothers' hatred toward Joseph, which eventually led to his killing. Even up to that moment, Jacob's favoritism still persisted. In the famine, Jacob sent the ten brothers to buy grain but kept Benjamin at home. When the brothers reported that Benjamin might have to come along the next time they visited Egypt,

Struggle with God and Overcome

Jacob refused. Even when Reuben pledged his two sons as a guarantee, Jacob still held on to Benjamin, "My son will not go down there with you; his brother is dead and he is the only one left. If harm comes to him on the journey you are taking, you will bring my gray head down to the grave in sorrow" (Gen 42:37–38). On the contrary, when the brothers came home without Simeon, Jacob grieved but delayed getting Simeon back, for the fear that harm would come to Benjamin, as Judah disclosed in their arguments, "If we had not delayed, we could have gone and returned twice" (Gen 43:10).

In Joseph's case, the brothers vented their anger and successfully got rid of him. To cover up, they had to kill a goat to bloodstain Joseph's robe and tell a lie to Jacob. Now in Egypt, the setup to get rid of another favorite son, Benjamin, was perfectly prepared for them. Joseph told the brothers to go home but to leave Benjamin in Egypt. The brothers had a ready-made excuse to avenge their father's favoritism and would not need to lie about it. But now, Judah, who suggested selling Joseph to the Ishmaelites, pleaded to take Benjamin's place.

> Your servant my father said to us, "You know that my wife bore me two sons. One of them went away from me, and I said, 'He has surely been torn to pieces.' And I have not seen him since. If you take this one from me too and harm comes to him, you will bring my gray head down to the grave in misery."
> So now, if the boy is not with us when I go back to your servant my father, and if my father, whose life is closely bound up with the boy's life, sees that the boy isn't there, he will die. Your servants will bring the gray head of our father down to the grave in sorrow. Your servant guaranteed the boy's safety to my father. I said, "If I do not bring him back to you, I will bear the blame before you, my father, all my life!"
> Now then, please let your servant remain here as my lord's slave in place of the boy, and let the boy return with his brothers. How can I go back to my father if the boy is not with me? No! Do not let me see the misery that would come on my father. (Gen 44:27–34)

Second Reunion

Furthermore, Judah's attitude, as well as the brothers', changed toward their father. In the past, they had not only taken away Jacob's favorite son but also deceived him of Joseph's disappearance. Now Judah was not afraid to repeat Jacob's words about the sons; "my wife bore me two sons." "If my father, whose life is closely bound up with the boy's life, sees that the boy isn't there, he will die." These statements hurt the feelings of the other ten brothers: they were also his sons. They forgave their father's partiality and pleaded not only for Benjamin but also for Jacob: "Do not let me see the misery that would come on my father."

At that point, Joseph could no longer control himself. He asked all attendants to leave and made himself known to his brothers.

> I am your brother Joseph, the one you sold into Egypt! And now, do not be distressed and do not be angry with yourselves for selling me here, because it was to save lives that God sent me ahead of you. For two years now there has been famine in the land, and for the next five years there will be no plowing and reaping. But God sent me ahead of you to preserve for you a remnant on earth and to save your lives by a great deliverance. (Gen 45:4–7)

Joseph revealed his true identity, and all the brothers recognized him, although stunned. Joseph forgave the brothers' wrongdoing and pointed out that God planned to save the family.

> You can see for yourselves, and so can my brother Benjamin, that it is really I who am speaking to you. Tell my father about all the honor accorded me in Egypt and about everything you have seen. (Gen 45:12–13)

Some scholars considered Joseph prideful in telling the brothers that "all the honor accorded me in Egypt and about everything you have seen." In the light that Joseph's life symbolizes Jesus, this statement can only be truthful and fitting for Jesus.

> Then he threw his arms around his brother Benjamin and wept, and Benjamin embraced him, weeping. And he kissed all his brothers and wept over them. Afterward his brothers talked with him ... To each of them he gave

new clothing, but to Benjamin he gave three hundred shekels of silver and five sets of clothes. (Gen 45:14, 22)

Joseph had a special affection for Benjamin, calling him out, throwing arms around him, and giving him more silver and clothes. A simple reason is that both of them had the same parents. However, their relationship has a more profound implication when the role of Benjamin is understood.

> So they went up out of Egypt and came to their father Jacob in the land of Canaan. They told him, "Joseph is still alive! In fact, he is ruler of all Egypt." Jacob was stunned; he did not believe them. But when they told him everything Joseph had said to them, and when he saw the carts Joseph had sent to carry him back, the spirit of their father Jacob revived. And Israel said, "I'm convinced! My son Joseph is still alive. I will go and see him before I die." (Gen 45:25–28)

This moment is the climax of Jacob's life, and the message is simple and clear: "Joseph is still alive."

The highlights of the second reunion are summarized as follows: First, the silver was returned a second time. Second, Judah acknowledged that God uncovered their guilt on Joseph, and their repentance led to a changed attitude toward Benjamin, another favorite son of Jacob. Third, Judah pleaded to take his place when commanded to leave without Benjamin. That is, the ten brothers accepted Benjamin as one of their own. Fourth, Joseph revealed his true identity and forgave the brothers. Finally, Jacob knew Joseph was still alive.

Second Reunion

Signature Traits of the Second Reunion

1	Again, their silvers were returned.
2	Judah acknowledged their guilt on Joseph.
3	Judah pleaded for Benjamin.
4	Joseph revealed himself and the brothers accepted him.
5	All knew Joseph was alive.

Table 10. Characteristics of the second reunion

Benjamin

WHO WAS BENJAMIN? WHY did he get five times the portion at the second reunion banquet, 300 shekels of silver, and five sets of clothes? Why did Joseph plant a cup only in his sack? Why must Benjamin come to Egypt to allow the brothers to see Joseph's face again? Joseph called him out at the reunion, embraced, and wept with him. If Judah signified the nation of Israel, and Joseph as Jesus, who did Benjamin signify?

These questions can be addressed from three perspectives: the cup in his sack, the close brotherhood with Joseph, and the mandate that Benjamin must come on the second trip.

Of the eleven brothers, only Benjamin got the cup. The cup had a special meaning for Joseph: Pharaoh's cupbearer was forgiven and restored, while the baker was hung. As discussed above, the cup, associated with wine, connotes spirit and forgiveness. Thus, Benjamin having the cup symbolizes the spirit and forgiveness that reside in Benjamin.

Next, Benjamin is Joseph's full brother and, because Joseph foreshadows Jesus, Benjamin is representative of Jesus' brothers. When someone told Jesus that his mother and brothers were standing outside, wanting to speak to him, Jesus replied, "Who is my mother, and who are my brothers?" Pointing to his disciples, he said, "Here are my mother and my brothers. For whoever does the will of my Father in heaven is my brother and sister and mother" (Matt 12:47–50).

BENJAMIN

Finally, on the first trip, Joseph mandated to the brothers that "you will not see my face again unless your brother is with you." That is, Benjamin must meet with Joseph before Judah and his brothers could. In our parallel model of Joseph as Jesus and Judah and his brothers as Jews, Benjamin represents the group that will come to Jesus before the Jews will in the second coming. In this, the apostle Paul provides a clue. "Until the full number of the Gentiles has come in, and in this way all Israel will be saved" (Rom 11:25–26).

All these clues indicate that Benjamin symbolizes gentile Christians, who have been forgiven, given the Holy Spirit, and are called the brothers of Jesus. This reading is consistent with Benjamin's absence in the first reunion because the gentile Christian group had not existed in Jesus' first coming in which Jesus came for the lost sheep of Israel. Now in the second coming, gentile Christians will play a central role. The full number of gentile Christians will gate the salvation of Jews, as the apostle Paul wrote. Further, Judah's plea for Benjamin is tantamount to Jews accepting gentile Christians and hence Jesus. Thus, Joseph's edict of Benjamin coming before the brothers could see his face parallels with Jesus' warning to the Jewish leaders that "you will not see me again until you say, 'Blessed is he who comes in the name of the Lord'" (Matt 23:39). In conclusion, Joseph's clan, consisting of Joseph and Benjamin, heralds Jesus and all gentile Christian believers.

Second Coming

THE CLOSE SIMILARITIES OF the signature traits between Joseph's first reunion and Jesus' first coming inevitably suggest the second reunion foreshadows Jesus' second coming, a prophetic message that has yet to be fulfilled.

First, a common thread in both reunions is that the silver was returned. In light of the New Testament, "all are justified freely by his grace through the redemption that came by Christ Jesus" (Rom 3:24), the twice returns of silver emphasize the grace of God in the two instances. In the words of Joseph when he interpreted Pharaoh's dream, "The reason the dream was given to Pharaoh in *two* forms is that the matter has been firmly decided by God, and God will do it soon" (Gen 41:32).

Second, Judah acknowledged that God uncovered their sins on Joseph, and they repented as evidenced by their protection of Benjamin. In Jesus' ministry, he preached repentance as the prerequisite for salvation. "From that time on Jesus began to preach, 'Repent, for the kingdom of heaven has come near'" (Matt 4:17). "But unless you repent, you too will all perish" (Luke 13:3, 5). If the second reunion foreshadows the second coming of Jesus, Judah is symbolic of the nation of Israel, and Joseph is symbolic of Jesus, Judah's remorse signifies the repentance of the nation of Israel that leads to their salvation, as the apostle Paul states, "Israel has experienced a hardening in part until the full number of the Gentiles has come in, and in this way all Israel will be saved" (Rom 11:25–26).

Third, Judah and the brothers' acceptance of Benjamin as their own signifies Jews' acceptance of Christians and hence Jesus in the second coming. Jesus once proclaimed, "You will not see me again until you say, 'Blessed is he who comes in the name of the Lord'" (Matt 23:39). On the day that his brothers sold Joseph, he was sent by their father Jacob to "see if all is well with your brothers and with the flocks, and bring word back to me" (Gen 37:14). At that time, Judah and the brothers rejected Joseph. Similarly, on the second trip to Egypt, Benjamin was sent by their father so that they could buy grain. Judah and the other brothers could simply follow Joseph's edict and leave Benjamin there if they wanted to reject him as they did to Joseph. Judah's plea demonstrated their acceptance of Benjamin as their brother. Benjamin was the second chance for Judah's clan to redeem themselves. Therefore, Jews will accept Jesus and Christians in the second coming.

Fourth, Joseph revealed his true identity in the second union, and his brothers received him. By the same token, in Jesus' second coming, Jews will recognize and receive Jesus. As the apostle Paul wrote in Romans 11:25–32:

> Israel has experienced a hardening in part until the full number of the Gentiles has come in, and in this way all Israel will be saved. As it is written:
> "The deliverer will come from Zion;
>   he will turn godlessness away from Jacob.
> And this is my covenant with them
>   when I take away their sins."
> As far as the gospel is concerned, they are enemies for your sake; but as far as election is concerned, they are loved on account of the patriarchs, for God's gifts and his call are irrevocable. Just as you who were at one time disobedient to God have now received mercy as a result of their disobedience, so they too have now become disobedient in order that they too may now receive mercy as a result of God's mercy to you. For God has bound everyone over to disobedience so that he may have mercy on them all.

Joseph forgave the brothers and told them that God sent him ahead of them to save their lives. Similarly, on the cross, Jesus said, "Father, forgive them, for they do not know what they are doing" (Luke 23:34). When Jesus' disciples were troubled by Jesus' prediction of his death, leaving the disciples, Jesus consoled them, "If I go and prepare a place for you, I will come back and take you to be with me that you also may be where I am" (John 14:3).

Finally, Jacob and the brothers exclaimed, "Joseph is still alive!" This proclamation is the crowning moment for Jesus. Jesus rose from death and is alive! Further, "God made me [Joseph] father to Pharaoh, lord of this entire household and ruler of all Egypt" (Gen 45:8). Similarly, in Galilee with his disciples, Jesus declared, "All authority in heaven and on earth has been given to me" (Matt 28:18).

	Joseph and Brothers' Second Reunion	Jesus' Second Coming
1	Again, their silvers were returned.	Grace from God.
2	Judah acknowledged their guilt on Joseph.	Jews will repent for Jesus.
3	Judah pleaded for Benjamin.	Jews will receive gentile Christians because of Jesus.
4	Joseph revealed himself and the brothers accepted him.	Jews will accept Jesus as the Messiah.
5	All knew Joseph was alive.	All will proclaim Jesus is alive.

Table 11. Comparison of the second reunion and Jesus' second coming

A diagram showing the matching signature traits between the second union and Jesus' second coming is in figure 10. Joseph, Benjamin, and Judah and brothers signify Jesus, gentile Christians, and Jews, respectively. The events in the second reunion mirror those in Jesus's second coming.

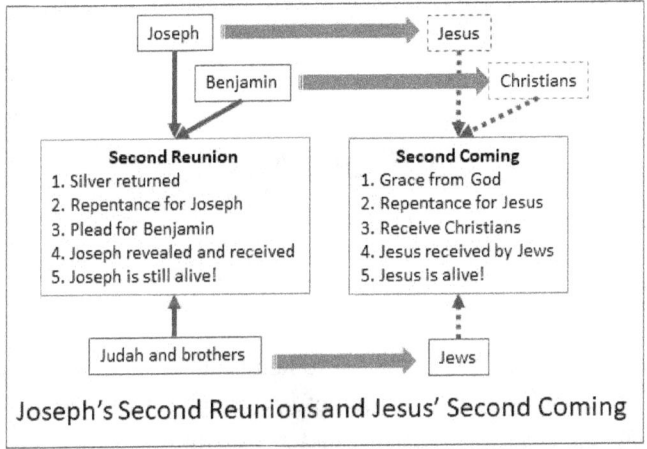

Figure 10. Comparing Joseph's second reunion with Jesus' second coming.

In conclusion, the second union between Joseph and his brothers is a prophetic meeting about Jesus' second coming. It depicts the future salvation of the nation of Israel and its unity with gentile Christian believers, the pinnacle of God's salvation plan. "For he himself is our peace, who has made the two groups one and has destroyed the barrier, the dividing wall of hostility, by setting aside in his flesh the law with its commands and regulations. His purpose was to create in himself one new humanity out of the two, thus making peace" (Eph 2:14–15).

Motif and Auspice

JUDAH'S AND JOSEPH'S CLANS have significant spiritual representations. Judah's clan is the nation of Israel under the law and judgment. The story of Judah and Tamar is the motif characteristic of the nation of Israel. Based on their deeds, Er and Onan were judged wicked and Tamar, righteous. Joseph's clan is the nation of grace. All are under the wrath of God and deserve death, but salvation comes by grace, not by deeds. The story of the cupbearer and the baker is the motif representative of this nation of God. Both the cupbearer and the baker under the wrath of Pharaoh were in prison. By providence, the cupbearer was saved, illustrating the underlying spiritual principle: spirit gives life. Benjamin symbolizes this nation of God, the gentile Christian believers saved by the spirit.

Hundreds of years before Jesus, the two reunions between Judah and Joseph prophesize the historical first coming and the future second coming of Jesus in exacting detail. In Jesus' first coming, the gentile Christian group had not existed during Jesus' ministry, as Jesus came to save first the Israelites, and this fact was reflected in Benjamin's absence in the first reunion. As the brothers did not recognize Joseph, the Jews did not recognize Jesus as their Messiah. As Joseph prompted the brothers of their wrongdoings, Jesus preached repentance. As Joseph predicated the second trip to Egypt on Benjamin, Jesus assured that Israelites would not see him again until they acknowledged him. Just as the brothers were bewildered to learn the return of silver, Israelites still believed

Motif and Auspice

in deeds, not grace. In Jesus' second coming, as foretold in Joseph's second reunion, Jesus will open the eyes of Israelites, and they will recognize him as the resurrected Messiah. Israelites will accept Jesus and receive Christian believers.

Figure 11 captures the signature traits and auspice of the life stories of Judah and Joseph, illustrating Joseph's mission in Egypt as the foreshadowing of Jesus' ministry and God's salvation plan for Israelites and gentiles. The top half of the box represents the New Testament era: salvation by grace. The shaded bottom half represents the Old Testament era: righteousness by deeds. The key figures in the Old Testament era are Judah and his brothers, who symbolize the nation of Israel. The story of Judah and Tamar is the motif story of law and judgment. In the New Testament era, the key figures are Joseph and Benjamin, who herald Jesus and the gentile Christian believers, respectively. The story of the cupbearer and baker is the motif story of salvation by grace. The two reunions between Joseph and his brothers are symbolic of the two comings of Jesus and the reconciliation between Jews and Jesus and gentile Christians. The thick horizontal arrows denote parallel counterparts. The middle four boxes list the signature traits tying the first reunion with the first coming, and the second reunion with the second coming.

STRUGGLE WITH GOD AND OVERCOME

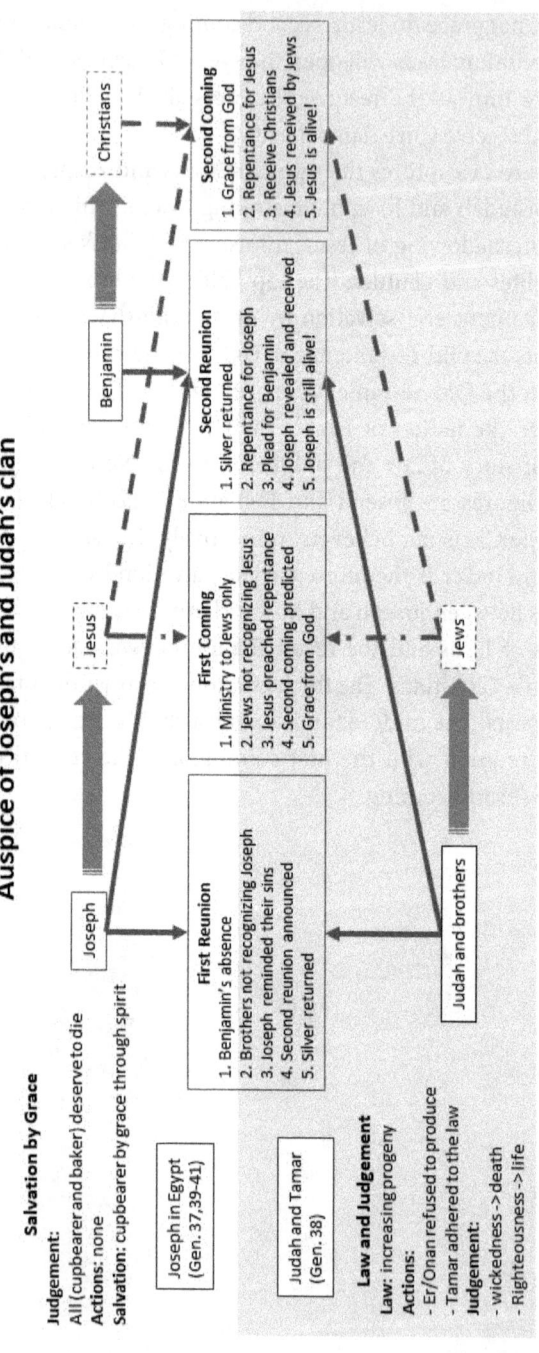

Figure 11. Spiritual implications of Joseph's and Judah's clan

The Wrestled Blessing

NOW, WE RETURN TO the original question of what the blessing was when Jacob insisted on getting one at the end of the wrestling match. The blessing can be inferred from the events in the period from the wrestling match to when Jacob reunited with Joseph, namely, the mission years. The mission years, i.e., the second and third stages of Jacob's life, are self-contained, i.e., one event led to another until it reached a closure when the family reunited in Egypt. Referring to Jacob's life summary, repeated here in figure 12, this blessing lasted for thirty-three years, from age ninety-seven to age 130, when he entered Egypt.

Jacob's mission years have multiple incidents: the test of the elected, tribes forming, clan bifurcation, message formation, and reunions. The incident at Shechem has tested the family as the elected people of God. The tribes have completed their formation at Rachel's death and Reuben's indiscretion. The birth of daughter Dinah divides the twelves sons into two clans. The first ten sons form a clan headed by Judah, and the next two sons, another clan headed by Joseph. This moment marks the end of stage 2. At the beginning of stage 3, the tribe formation is completed, and the heads of the two clans branch out from the family, when Joseph was sold to Egypt and Judah left for Canaan. Next, the two clans take up different paths, living out the respective messages the clans symbolize, the central theological themes in the Bible. Judah's clan foreshadows the nation of Israel, embodying righteousness by the law, whereas

Joseph's clan, the Christian believers, embodies salvation through grace. The reunions of the two clans foretell the grand finale of God's salvation plan for humanity.

The development of Jacob's family along with the major events and their key messages in Jacob's mission years are summarized in figure 13. Jacob's mission years are segmented into two at the branching of the two clans.

The nexus between Jacob's mission years and God's overall salvation plan has been established through parallel identification of the main characters and their interplays, which are summarized in figure 14.

In figure 14, the lower left box "Jacob's Wrestled Blessing" represents the iconic development of the events in Jacob's family since the wrestling. Benjamin came into the picture only after the first reunion. The upper right box "God's Plan Heralded" represents the key events in Jesus' ministry. Christians came into the picture only after the first coming. The lower right box summarizes the evidence that links Judah's clan to the nation of Israel. Similarly, the upper left box lists seven key attributes present in Joseph's and Jesus' life and thus establish the character parallel linkage. The middle box lists the seven key messages in the two reunions that establish event parallel linkage between the reunions and the comings. Once these major correspondences are anchored, the other linkages are implicitly established by their positions within the boxes, such as Benjamin to Christians, first reunion to first coming, and second reunion to second coming.

Therefore, Jacob's mission years live out a microcosm of God's salvation plan, resonating prophetically the main messages of the Bible. (1) God chose the nation of Israel as his people. (2) God introduced law and judgment. (3) The elected people failed under the law. (4) God sent Jesus to save by grace, (5) Jesus resurrected and triumphed over death, (6) the nation of Israel failed to recognize Jesus and the grace went to all who believe, namely, Christians, and (7) finally, all Israel will come to recognize and receive Jesus and be saved.

The Wrestled Blessing

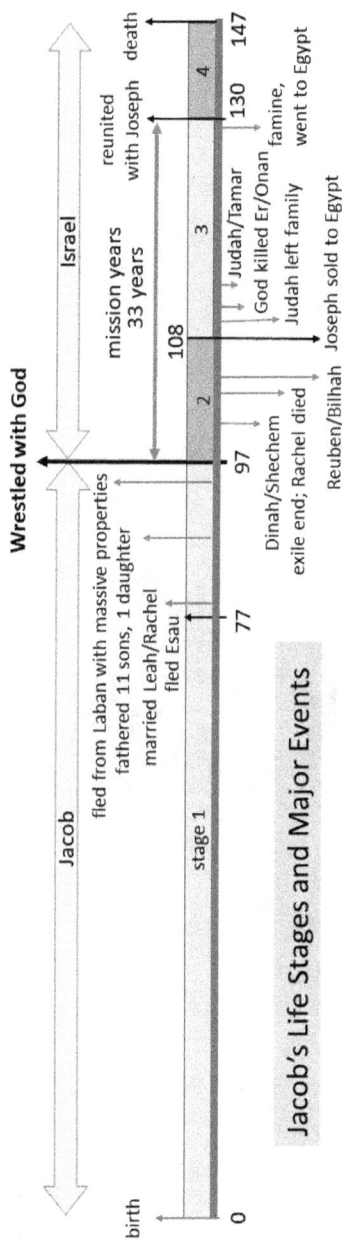

Figure 12. Jacob's life summary

STRUGGLE WITH GOD AND OVERCOME

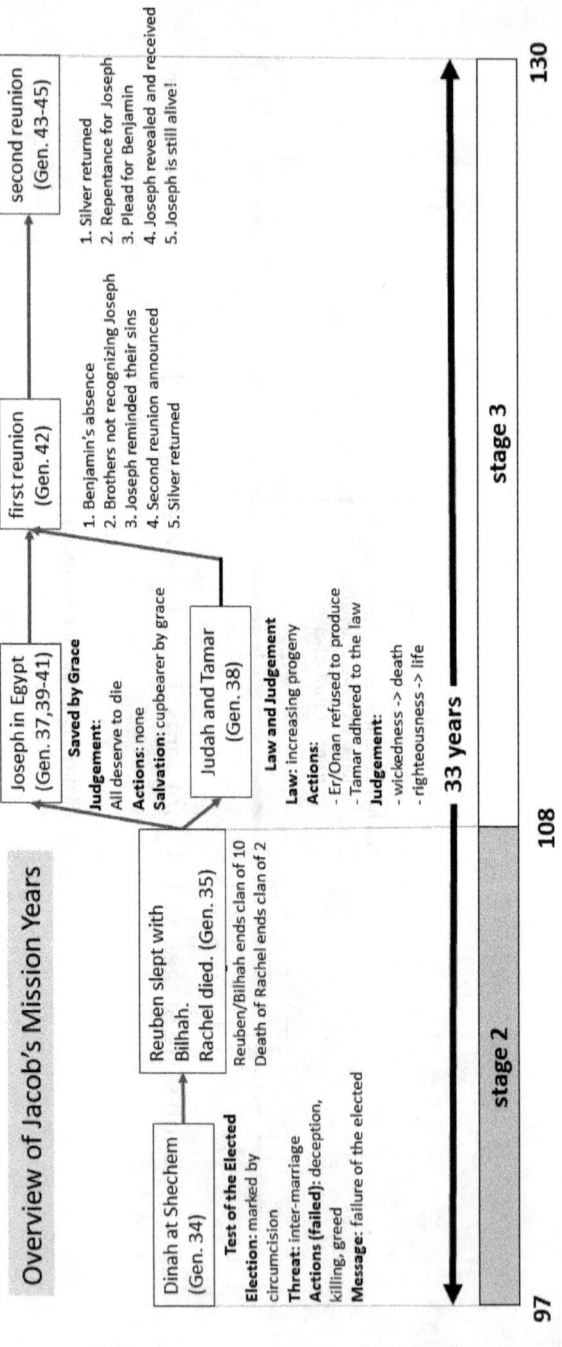

Figure 13. Major events in Jacob's mission years

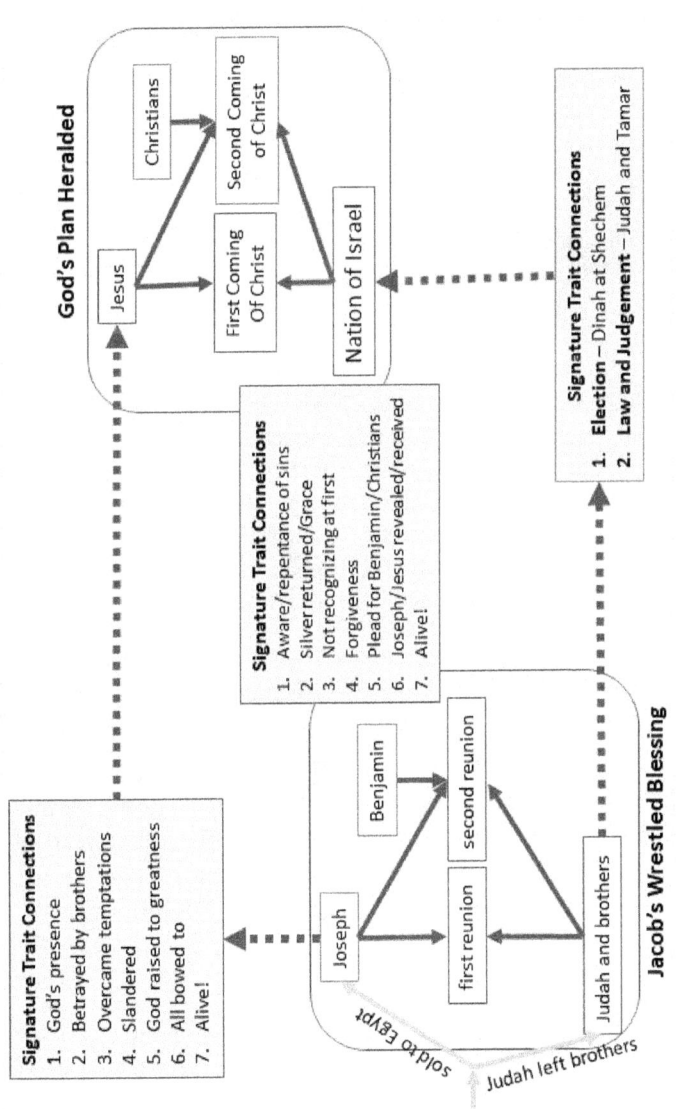

Figure 14. Significance of Jacob's mission years

Now God's salvation plan has been revealed to all, as the apostle Paul wrote succinctly and cogently:

> No one will be declared righteous in God's sight by the works of the law; rather, through the law we become conscious of our sin. But now apart from the law the righteousness of God has been made known, to which the Law and the Prophets testify. This righteousness is given through faith in Jesus Christ to all who believe.
>
> . . .
>
> But concerning Israel he says,
> "All day long I have held out my hands
> to a disobedient and obstinate people."
>
> . . .
>
> Israel has experienced a hardening in part until the full number of the Gentiles has come in, and in this way all Israel will be saved. As it is written:
> "The deliverer will come from Zion;
> he will turn godlessness away from Jacob.
> And this is my covenant with them
> when I take away their sins."
> (Rom 3:20–22; 10:21; 11:25–27)

In summary, what is the wrestled blessing? The wrestled blessing has fully manifested in Jacob's mission years, which—thirty-three years in all—is a singular point in history that has expanded into millennia of God's salvation and is still continuing until Jesus comes again. Jacob was blessed to live out a condensed version of God's salvation plan for all humanity. The thirty-three years of Jacob's mission years—matching Jesus' time on earth—serves as a reminder of the revelation of God's salvation as the ultimate blessing in Jacob's life.

Patriarchal Narratives

Is THE ABOVE READING of Jacob's mission years intended by the author? This is just one of many Old Testament stories that tell about Jesus. To Jewish leaders, Jesus said, "You study the Scriptures diligently because you think that in them you have eternal life. These are the very Scriptures that testify about me, yet you refuse to come to me to have life" (John 5:39–40). After the resurrection and on the road to Emmaus, Jesus spoke to two disciples about the Scripture. Beginning with Moses and all the prophets, Jesus explained to them what was said in all the Scriptures concerning himself (Luke 24:27).

In this broad sense, this reading is consistent with the main purposes of the scripture, as Jesus stated. A deeper question is: does it fit well with the spiritual context and development of Jacob's and his ancestors' time? It is probable that Jacob was not fully aware of the spiritual ramifications of his thirty-three years of struggle on the grand scale of God's plan. Nevertheless, being a patriarch, Jacob's life should have as much spiritual significance as Abraham's and Isaac's. Furthermore, it is imperative that the spiritual nature and significance of Jacob's mission years dovetail with the spiritual narratives of the lives of Abraham and Isaac because God started his salvific plan with these three patriarchs. Then, what are the key spiritual narratives in Abraham's life? To this, the apostle Paul has argued extensively in chapter 4 of Romans that Abraham's life exemplifies one important spiritual principle: Abraham is credited as righteous through faith, and through the righteousness he received God's promise of grace. Regarding righteousness through faith, Paul contends that Abraham sets the example that righteousness comes to anyone who believes, circumcised or not, not because he follows the law of circumcision.

> We have been saying that Abraham's faith was credited to him as righteousness. Under what circumstances was it credited? Was it after he was circumcised, or before? It was not after, but before! And he received circumcision as a sign, a seal of the righteousness that he had by faith while he was still uncircumcised. So then, he is the father of all who believe but have not been circumcised, in order that righteousness might be credited to them. And he is then also the father of the circumcised who not only are circumcised but who also follow in the footsteps of the faith that our father Abraham had before he was circumcised. (Rom 4:9–12)

Then, God's promise comes to Abraham as a result of the righteousness. "It was not through the law that Abraham and his offspring received the promise that he would be heir of the world, but through the righteousness that comes by faith" (Rom 4:13). "Therefore, the promise comes by faith, so that it may be by grace and may be guaranteed to all Abraham's offspring—not only to those who are of the law but also to those who have the faith of Abraham. He is the father of us all" (Rom 4:16).

To sum it up, the spiritual narratives of Abraham's life, centering around the issue of faith versus law and grace versus work, establish the foundation of righteousness by faith and that righteousness begets the promise of grace for all Jews and gentiles. Grounded in this foundation, Jacob's mission years personify the narratives: one nation under grace and the other under the law, which eventually arrives at salvation through faith in Jesus. Further, Jacob's mission years outline a symbolical blueprint according to which the salvation plan unfolds. In this way, this reading of Jacob's mission years conforms to and extends the spiritual narratives of Abraham's life.

Tribal Blessings

NEAR THE END OF his life, Jacob told his sons of their future, shedding more light on the three protagonists, Judah, Joseph, and Benjamin. His blessings touched upon some tribal history but also carried a heavy prophetic message, as Jacob said to his son, "Gather around so I can tell you what will happen to you in days to come" (Gen 49:1). For Benjamin, a beloved son dear to his heart, Jacob's blessing seemed to be incongruous, calling him a ravenous wolf, an astonishing metaphor for a family of shepherds. In fact, the heavily prophetic contents of Jacob's final words prove valuable in strengthening the above parallel analysis for Judah, Joseph, and Benjamin.

For Judah, Jacob blessed:

> Judah, your brothers will praise you;
>   your hand will be on the neck of your enemies;
>   your father's sons will bow down to you.
> You are a lion's cub, Judah;
>   you return from the prey, my son.
> Like a lion he crouches and lies down,
>   like a lioness—who dares to rouse him.
> The scepter will not depart from Judah,
>   nor the ruler's staff from between his feet,
> until he to whom it belongs shall come
>   and the obedience of the nations shall be his.
> He will tether his donkey to a vine,
>   his colt to the choicest branch;

> he will wash his garments in wine,
>> his robes in the blood of grapes.
> His eyes will be darker than wine,
>> his teeth whiter than milk. (Gen 49:8–12)

Three features stand out here: bowing of his brothers, the scepter, and vine/wine. As understood in the context of Joseph's dream, the bowing of his brothers establishes Judah as the head of the family or nation of Israel. The scepter invokes the image of kings coming from Judah and his descendants ("between his feet"). Because a nation is symbolized by its kings, this message further supports Judah's tribe to lead the nation of Israel. Kingship will continue within Judah's lineage until "he to whom it belongs shall come and the obedience of the nations shall be his." In hindsight, it is clear that the kingship eventually belongs to Jesus, who came from the tribe of Judah, to whom all nations will be subjected. This transition of kingship opens the door for interpreting the following verses about vine, branch, wine, and blood of the grape. The latter part of Judah's blessings is tied to Joseph's because Joseph's blessing starts with "Joseph is a fruitful vine." Further, Jesus declared, "I am the true vine" (John 15:1). Thus, this part of the blessing confirms that Joseph foreshadows Jesus and that the nation of Israel will eventually come to Jesus, as "he will tether his donkey to a vine, his colt to the choicest branch." Wine in context represents the spirit, and washing of clothes connotes the cleansing of sins. "He will wash his garments in wine, his robes in the blood of grapes." The nation of Israel will return, cleansing their sins through the blood of Jesus.

For Joseph, Jacob blessed:

> Joseph is a fruitful vine,
>> a fruitful vine near a spring,
>> whose branches climb over a wall.
> With bitterness archers attacked him;
>> they shot at him with hostility.
> But his bow remained steady,
>> his strong arms stayed limber,
>> because of the hand of the Mighty One of Jacob,
>> because of the Shepherd, the Rock of Israel,

> because of your father's God, who helps you,
>   because of the Almighty, who blesses you
> with blessings of the skies above,
>   blessings of the deep springs below,
>   blessings of the breast and womb.
> Your father's blessings are greater
>   than the blessings of the ancient mountains,
>   than the bounty of the age-old hills.
> Let all these rest on the head of Joseph,
>   on the brow of the prince among his brothers.
> (Gen 49:22–26)

Again, three features stand out here: Joseph is a vine, he was attacked, but by the hand of God all blessings rest on him. Jesus said that he is the true vine. Jesus was attacked and nailed to the cross. Joseph was sustained by the hand of the Mighty One, the Shepherd, the Rock of Israel. By the hand of the almighty God, Jesus rose from death. Like the "blessings of the skies above, blessings of the deep springs below, . . . let all these rest on the head of Joseph," Jesus declared, "All authority in heaven and on earth has been given to me" (Matt 28:18). Therefore, Joseph's blessings herald those of Jesus.

Judah's blessing reveals a kingdom that lasts through his descendants until the One has come, but God is absent in the kingdom. By contrast, Joseph's blessing is filled with God's presence: the Mighty One, the Shepherd, the Rock of Israel, your father's God, and the Almighty. Thus, Judah's kingdom is on earth, Joseph's, a kingdom in heaven. For Judah, all brothers would bow to him. For Joseph, the first version of his bowing dream (sheaves) was fulfilled when the brothers came to Egypt, but his second version of the bowing dream was not fulfilled where celestial objects bowed to him. This celestial bowing dream is superior to the sheaves version and could only be fulfilled on Jesus because Joseph projects the image of Jesus.

In the biblical patriarchal tradition, the dying patriarch blesses the firstborn. To Jacob, Joseph was his firstborn because Rachel was the woman he wanted to marry first. So, Jacob gave Joseph, not Judah, the patriarchal blessing and twice the portion of land as any other brother (Gen 48:15–22). That was a historical moment because the patriarchal blessing had passed symbolically from earth to heaven. Because Joseph's kingdom is a kingdom of heaven, events from Joseph's tribe have been left out of future Jewish annals. For the same reason, Judah's tribe has occupied the central position in future Jewish annals.

Benjamin's blessing is most intriguing and incongruous, comparing the youngest and dearest son to a ravenous wolf, whose image is surely not lovely to shepherds.

> Benjamin is a ravenous wolf;
> in the morning he devours the prey,
> in the evening he divides the plunder. (Gen 49:27)

The above discussion led to the conclusion that Benjamin represented gentile Christians. How can we harmonize this benediction? Some scholars have pointed out that the apostle Paul, of the Benjamin tribe, was like a ravenous wolf in his early years, persecuting Christians, but after his conversion, Paul fed the church with his spiritual teachings. This interpretation has touched upon the connection with gentile Christians, as Paul himself declared to be the apostle for gentiles. However, the parallel of Benjamin should be more than just an individual.

Is there another reading of this blessing that links to the gentile Christian community? To shepherds, wolves are enemies of sheep; wolves are not a part of the family. When dispatching his disciples to preach, Jesus said, "I am sending you out like sheep among wolves" (Matt 10:16). Gentiles are not a part of the elected people and thus are like wolves outside of the sheep pen. But through faith in Jesus Christ, gentiles have become a part of God's family. "But now apart from the law the righteousness of God has been made known, to which the Law and the Prophets testify. This righteousness is given through faith in Jesus Christ to all who believe. There is no difference between Jew and Gentile" (Rom 3:21–22).

Whose plunder is it that Benjamin divides? Jesus explained that he drove out demons by the Spirit of God as a house would be

Tribal Blessings

plundered if the house is not guarded by a strong man (Mark 3:27). Jesus has "disarmed the powers and authorities, he made a public spectacle of them, triumphing over them by the cross" (Col 2:15). Therefore, in Benjamin's blessing, the morning and evening denote before and after. Before gentile Christians were not a part of God's family, like wolves outside of the sheep pen, but now, through faith in Jesus Christ, Christians have joined the family and shared the plunders from Jesus' victory over all powers and authorities. In the evening, the wolf will live with the lamb (Isa 11:6). Therefore, Benjamin's blessing is a fitting description of gentile Christians' standing in history.

Hence, Joseph and Benjamin form one clan symbolic of the spiritual nation of Israel, while Judah and the other brothers represent the earthly nation of Israel. Interestingly, a similar subdivision within Joseph's clan continues: the clan has twelve sons—Joseph has two, and Benjamin, ten. A possible interpretation is that the number ten confirms a corporate body that Benjamin symbolizes.

In summary, Jacob's blessings of his sons reinforce the interpretation of Judah, Joseph, and Benjamin in the light of the New Testament.

Struggle with God and Overcome

IF GOD COULD CRIPPLE Jacob with a mere touch on his hip, why was Jacob told that he struggled with God and had overcome in the wrestling match? Could anyone possibly overcome God at all?

The man in the wrestling match said to Jacob, "Your name will no longer be Jacob, but Israel because you have struggled with God and with humans and have overcome" (Gen 32:28). Why would Jacob's name need to be changed because of the wrestling match? In the Bible, a name is changed to reflect a person's changed life as a result of a covenant. For example, God asked Abram to change his name to Abraham to commemorate the covenant that he would be "a father of many nations." Hence, changing the name Jacob to Israel—as the names imply—signifies the transition from struggling with people in the past to struggling with God and overcoming in the years ahead. Thus, the statement "struggled with God and have overcome" has dual meanings: one for the present wrestling match and the other, a prophetic message for the years ahead. At the match, Jacob wrestled and won the blessing from God. In the following years, how then did Jacob struggle with God and overcome? To decipher the statement, break it into two parts: "struggle with God" and "overcome."

What did Jacob struggle with God? In hindsight, the answer is more apparent. God blessed Jacob with the task of living out the microcosm of his salvation plan, which involved brutal truths such as the failures of the elected, sin and judgment, and the sufferings

Struggle with God and Overcome

characteristic of the Messiah. The hardships were necessary to reflect humanity's sinful and dilapidated state. Jacob struggled with the rape of his only daughter, Dinah, the deceit and violence of his two sons, Simeon and Levi, and the massacre of many innocent people in Shechem. Jacob struggled with the death of his beloved wife Rachel and the disdain of his firstborn, Reuben. Jacob struggled with the death of his two grandsons. Jacob struggled with the disappearance of his favorite son, Joseph. All these were necessary and came from God. Jacob struggled with God.

Did he overcome God? No. God was too powerful for him—a touch wretched his hip socket. He did not overcome God because he asked for a blessing. Only the strong bless the weak. So, what did Jacob overcome? Jacob struggled with God and overcame the hardships. Jacob never lost faith in God. In his waning years, Jacob blessed Joseph,

> May the God before whom my fathers
> Abraham and Isaac walked faithfully,
> the God who has been my shepherd
> all my life to this day. (Gen 48:15)

After all the years that almost brought his gray head down to the grave with sorrow, Jacob called God his shepherd all his life to this day. Jacob overcame the hardships with steadfast faith in God.

Blessedness versus Happiness

IS THE WRESTLED BLESSING really a blessing? For Jacob, his mission years did not bring happiness but misery after misery that he thought he would go to "the grave in sorrow." When asked by Pharaoh about age, Jacob replied, "My years have been few and difficult, and they do not equal the years of the pilgrimage of my fathers" (Gen 47:9). The thirty-three years after the wrestling with God do not seem to be a blessing that Jacob sought. At the riverbank of Jabbok, Jacob's seeking of blessings was partly motivated by Esau's overwhelming presence and partly by the lack of evidence of his own even after being blessed by Isaac. He sought prosperity.

What is a blessing? A worldview definition would be a favored status with God, which endows power for prosperity and success. In this view, a blessing necessarily brings happiness. God blessed Abraham. Abraham became very wealthy in livestock and silver and gold (Gen 13:2). Abraham was militarily powerful. He rescued his nephew Lot from Kedorlaomer and the kings allied with him (Gen 14). Abraham was well protected. When the Pharaoh of Egypt took hold of Sarai, God inflicted serious diseases on Pharaoh and his household (Gen 12). And God warned Abimelek king of Gerar of his taking of Sarah (Gen 20). God blessed Isaac. Isaac planted crops and reaped a hundredfold. Isaac had so many flocks and herds and servants that the Philistines envied him (Gen 26). God blessed Jacob. Even though Laban was harsh, Jacob amassed so many properties that forced him to flee. Jacob faced

Blessedness versus Happiness

several life and death threats, but he escaped without harm. This worldview of blessing is what most people can relate to, and this notion of blessedness was the only kind for the patriarchs until Jacob's wrestled blessing.

Blessings come from God and are therefore under God's will. Within God's will, God empowers people to be prosperous and successful. As Moses announced to the Israelites, if you obey the Lord your God, "the Lord will open the heavens, the storehouse of his bounty, to send rain on your land in season and to bless all the work of your hands" (Deut 28:12). This worldview of blessing thus falls delightfully within most people's desire.

However, this is not all there is in God's will. God wants his people to be like him, "I am the Lord your God; consecrate yourselves and be holy, because I am holy" (Lev 11:44). The wrestled blessing transcends the worldview of blessedness beyond materialism into the spiritual realm by asserting fulfillment of God's will as the ultimate blessedness. The wrestled blessing fulfills the revelation of God's will to save humanity. In thirty-three years, it showcased, in a nutshell, the true spiritual state of humanity and detailed God's salvation plan. This elevated or spiritual view of blessing echoes with Jesus' teaching. Instead of prosperity and success, Jesus taught the disciples to pray for the fulfillment of God's will, "Our Father in heaven, hallowed be your name, your kingdom come, your will be done, on earth as it is in heaven" (Matt 6:9–10).

In this spiritual view, a blessing in fulfilling God's will at times contradicts the worldview of blessing, for the fundamental reason that God is holy, but people are sinful. There will be many occasions where God and we do not see eye to eye. To make people aware of sin, God gave laws and judged accordingly. On the one hand, it is blessed to be aware of sin and conscious of one's weakness to overcome and thus rely on God's grace. On the other hand, its biting truth seems to fall outside the worldview of blessing. Jesus captured this dilemma best in his beatitudes, "Blessed are the poor in spirit, for theirs is the kingdom of heaven" (Matt 5:3). In short, a blessing is not necessarily tantamount to happiness.

Struggle with God and Overcome

Therefore, blessings, especially those that touch spiritual reality, stir up the spirit and cause many to doubt God's benevolence. Until wrestling with God, Jacob had only experienced the worldview version of blessing. The night at the riverbank of Jabbok, Jacob was exposed to his weaknesses upon a mere touch on the hip, but he held on to "the Man" for blessing. For the first time, Jacob had to face his past wrongdoings, repent with humility, and let God deliver him from Esau. That encounter was a perfect setting to start Jacob's next thirty-three years of journey, embodying God's plan for all: weakness of humanity, repentance of sins, and salvation from God. The blessed hardship surprised Jacob. He struggled. The hardship challenged Jacob's faith in God's goodness. He preserved. In the end, Jacob overcame with faith and called God: "Who has been my shepherd all my life to this day" (Gen 48:15).

Bibliography

Andrew, M. E. "Moving from Death to Life: Verbs of Motion in the Story of Judah and Tamar in Gen 38." *Zeitschrift fur die Alttestamentliche Wissenschaft* 105 (1993) 262–69.

Armstrong, Karen. *In the Beginning*. New York: Knopf, 1996.

Auld, Graeme. "Tamar between David, Judah and Joseph." Paper delivered at Uppsala Exegetical Day, September 28, 1999.

Bakon, Shimon. "Subtleties in the Story of Joseph and Potiphar's Wife." *Jewish Bible Quarterly* 41 (2013) 171–74.

Bekins, Peter. "Tamar and Joseph in Genesis 38 and 39." *Journal for the Study of the Old Testament* 40 (2016) 375–97.

Carmichael, Calum. "Some Sayings in Genesis 49." *Journal of Biblical Literature* 88 (December 1969) 435–44.

Cohen, Jeffrey M. "Joseph and His Brothers: Sibling Rivalry Revisited." *Jewish Bible Quarterly* 49 (2021) 103–8.

Cohen, Jeremy. "The Mystery of Israel's Salvation: Romans 11:25–26 in Patristic and Medieval Exegesis." *Harvard Theological Review* 98 (July 2005) 247–81.

deClaisse-Walford, Nancy L. "Genesis 32:22–32: 'A Lonely Struggle and an Underserved Blessing.'" *Review and Expositor* 3 (2014) 74–77.

Doren, Mark Van. "Joseph and His Brothers: A Comedy in Four Parts." *American Scholar* 26 (Summer 1957) 289–302.

Edwards, Dennis. "Three Ways Old Testament Theology Points to Jesus." *N. T. Wright Online*, September 11, 2019. https://www.ntwrightonline.org/three-ways-old-testament-theology-points-to-jesus/.

Galadari, Abdulla. "Joseph and Jesus: Unearthing Symbolisms within the Bible and the Qur'an." *International Journal of Religion and Spirituality in Society* 1 (2011) 117–27.

Gardner, Joseph L., ed. *Atlas of the Bible*. Pleasantville, NY: Reader's Digest, 1981.

Gaventa, Bill. "Genesis 32:22–32." *Interpretation* 73 (2019) 386–88.

BIBLIOGRAPHY

Geller, Stephen A. "The Struggle at the Jabbok: The Uses of Enigma in a Biblical Narrative." *Journal of the Ancient Near Eastern Society* 14 (January 2019) 37–60.

Goldfarb, Solomon. "Was Simeon Not Included in Moses' Blessing?" *World Jewish Bible Society* 4 (1975) 51–55.

Golka, Friedemann W. "Genesis 37–50: Joseph Story or Israel-Joseph Story?" *Currents in Biblical Research* 2 (2004) 153–73.

Granot, Hayim. "Observations on the Character of Joseph in Egypt." *Jewish Bible Quarterly* 39 (2011) 263–67.

Green, Barbara. "God's Holy Spirit: A Backstory from the Joseph Narrative (Genesis 37–50)." *Acta Theologica Supplementum* 17 (2013) 25–49.

Greenberger, Chaya. "Esau and Jacob: Brothers Clash, Reconcile and Separate." *Jewish Bible Quarterly* 46 (2018) 143–57.

———. "Joseph and His Brothers: The Unexpected Encounter." *Jewish Bible Quarterly* 49 (2021) 158–64.

———. "Judah and Tamar: Self-Esteem Lost and (Partially) Redeemed." *Jewish Bible Quarterly* 48 (2020) 23–31.

———. "A Matter of Words and Assumptions in the Household of Jacob." *Jewish Bible Quarterly* 48 (2020) 143–56.

Grossman, Jonathan. "Different Dreams: Two Models of Interpretation for Three Pairs of Dreams (Genesis 37–50)." *Journal of Biblical Literature* (2016) 717–32.

Hamilton, James M. "Was Joseph a Type of the Messiah? Tracing the Typological Identification between Joseph, David, and Jesus." *Southern Baptist Journal of Theology* 12 (Winter 2008) 52–77.

Hannah, Darrell. "The Ravenous Wolf: The Apostle Paul and Genesis 49.27 in the Early Church." *New Testament Studies* 62 (October 2016) 610–27.

Hatzopoulos, Athanasios. "The Struggle for a Blessing: Reflections on Genesis 32:24–31." *Ecumenical Review* 48 (October 1996) 507–12.

Jacob's Travels. *iBible Maps*. https://ibiblemaps.com/jacobs-travels-2/.

Kass, Leon R. "Regarding Daughters and Sisters: The Rape of Dinah." *Commentary* 93 (April 1992) 29.

Kim, Dohyung. "The Structure of Genesis 38: A Thematic Reading." *Vetus Testamentum* 62 (2012) 550–60.

Kim, Eunjung. "A Parallel Structure between the Jacob Narrative (Gen 25:19—37:1) and the Joseph Narrative (Gen 37:2—50:26): The Purpose of God's Election of the Patriarch." Thesis submitted to the Faculty of Theology, University of St. Michael's College, and the Biblical Department, Toronto School of Theology, 2013.

Kim, Jae Gu. "The Literary Function of the Judah-Tamar Story (Gen. 38) in the Joseph Story." *Korean Journal of Christian Studies* 75 (2011) 43–60.

Krause, Joachim J. "Tradition, History, and Our Story: Some Observations on Jacob and Esau in the Books of Obadiah and Malachi." *Journal for the Study of the Old Testament* 32 (2008) 475–86.

Kruschwitz, Jonathan. "Tamar among the Matriarchs: Godless and Perhaps Closer to God." *Review and Expositor* 115 (2018) 542–55.

Bibliography

Kugel, James L. *The Ladder of Jacob: Ancient Interpretations of the Biblical Story of Jacob and His Children*. Princeton, NJ: Princeton University Press, 2006.

Lacey, Troy. "Jacob's Odd 'Breeding Program' of Genesis 30." *Answers in Genesis*, April 26, 2019. https://answersingenesis.org/genetics/animal-genetics/jacobs-odd-breeding-program-genesis-30/.

LaHaye, Tim. *Understanding the Last Days*. Eugene, OR: Harvest House, 1998.

Lett, Jonathan. "The Divine Identity of Jesus as the Reason for Israel's Unbelief in John 12:36–43." *Journal of Biblical Literature* 135 (Spring 2016) 159–73.

Levinson, Joshua. "An-Other Woman: Joseph and Potiphar's Wife; Staging the Body Politic." *Jewish Quarterly Review* 87 (January-April 1997) 269–301.

Lloyd-Jones, Martyn. *Studies in the Sermon on the Mount*. Grand Rapids: Eerdmans, 1959.

Lockyer, Herbert. *All the Parables of the Bible*. Grand Rapids: Zondervan, 1963.

Mann, Samuel J. "Joseph and His Brothers: A Biblical Paradigm for the Optimal Handling of Traumatic Stress." *Journal of Religion and Health* 40 (2001) 335–42.

Martens, Peter W. "Revisiting the Allegory/Typology Distinction: The Case of Origen." *Journal of Early Christian Studies* 16 (Fall 2008) 283–317.

Neufeld, Ernest. "The Rape of Dinah." *Jewish Bible Quarterly* 25 (January 1997) 220–24.

Newman, Stephen. "Pharaoh's Dreams: An Extended Interpretation." *Jewish Bible Quarterly* 40 (October-December 2012) 253–54.

Noegel, Scott B. "Sex, Sticks, and the Trickster in Gen. 30:31–43: A New Look at an Old Crux." *Journal of Ancient Near Eastern Society* 25 (1997) 7–17.

Peursen, Wido van. "Participant Reference in Genesis 37." *Journal of Northwest Semitic Languages* 39 (2013) 85–102.

Philpot, Joshua M. "Was Joseph a Type of Daniel? Typological Correspondence in Genesis 37–50 and Daniel 1–6." *Journal of the Evangelical Theological Society* (2018) 681–96.

Sailhamer, John H., et al., eds. *The Expositor's Bible Commentary*. Vol. 2. Grand Rapids: Zondervan, 1990.

Schimmel, Sol. "Joseph and His Brothers: A Paradigm for Repentance." *Judaism* 37 (1988) 60–65.

Sharon, Diane M. "Some Results of a Structural Semiotic Analysis of the Story of Judah and Tamar." *Journal for the Study of the Old Testament* 29 (2005) 289–318.

Snell, Robert T. "Genesis 32:22–32." *Interpretation* 50 (July 1996) 277–80.

Sonne, Isaiah. "Genesis 49:25–26." *Journal of Biblical Literature* (September 1946) 303–6.

Streed, Stephen. "The Jacob Factor: Aging and Spirituality." *Dialog* 58 (August 2019) 286–93.

Treves, Marco. "Shiloh (Genesis 49:10)." *Journal of Biblical Literature* (September 1966) 353–56.

Twersky, Geula. "Genesis 49: The Foundation of Israelite Monarchy and Priesthood." *Journal for the Study of the Old Testament* 43 (2019) 317–33.

BIBLIOGRAPHY

Weinberger, Theodore. "'And Joseph Slept with Potiphar's Wife': A Re-reading." *Literature and Theology* 11 (June 1997) 145–51.

Wildavsky, Aaron. "Survival Must Not Be Gained through Sin: The Moral of the Joseph Stories Prefigured through Judah and Tamar." *Journal for the Study of the Old Testament* 62 (1994) 37–48.

Yamada, Frank M. *Configurations of Rape in the Hebrew Bible: A Literary Analysis of Three Rape Narratives*. New York: Lang, 2008.

www.ingramcontent.com/pod-product-compliance
Lightning Source LLC
Chambersburg PA
CBHW071442160426
43195CB00013B/2001